D1163263

LOUISIANA
Sweets

KING CAKES, BREAD PUDDING & SWEET DOUGH PIE

DIXIE POCHÉ

AMERICAN PALATE

Published by American Palate
A division of The History Press
Charleston, SC
www.historypress.net

Copyright © 2017 by Dixie Poché

All rights reserved

Front cover, clockwise from top: Louisiana's state doughnut, the beignet. *Courtesy of the Louisiana Department of Culture, Recreation and Tourism*; country-style peach cobbler. *Courtesy of Del Monte Foods, Inc.*; blueberry pie. *Courtesy of the US Highbush Blueberry Council*; Bananas Foster pain perdu. *Courtesy of Elizabeth's Restaurant*; macaron cookies during carnival season at Sucre in New Orleans. *Courtesy of @hanafoto.*

Back cover, top: World-famous Café du Monde in New Orleans, 1939. *Courtesy of the Collections of the Louisiana State Museum*; *inset*: roi de gateaux, old-fashioned French king cake. *Courtesy of Travis Gauthier and Poupart's Bakery.*

First published 2017

ISBN 978-1-5402-2557-3

Library of Congress Control Number: 2017938338

Notice: The information in this book is true and complete to the best of our knowledge. It is offered without guarantee on the part of the author or The History Press. The author and The History Press disclaim all liability in connection with the use of this book.

All rights reserved. No part of this book may be reproduced or transmitted in any form whatsoever without prior written permission from the publisher except in the case of brief quotations embodied in critical articles and reviews.

Dedicated to my children, Roby and Renee.

Contents

Foreword

Of Louisiana's cultural assets that make the state known worldwide, its cuisine in all its varied and delicious forms is by far the proverbial jewel in the crown. The early French, African, Spanish, German, Hungarian, Italian and other settlers who made their homes in Louisiana brought with them their respective culinary traditions and preserved them in their old-world authenticity or enhanced them with ingredients and ideas unique to the New World. The result is an ongoing yet adaptable legacy of good cooking, attractive presentation and joyful consumption.

Many readers have fond memories of experiencing a form of affectionate "forced feeding" when visiting grandparents and other elders. Regardless if one had just eaten a full meal, he or she was expected to eat again, and the gastronomic victim was never disappointed by the proffered food and drink in which tradition and love were key ingredients.

In *Louisiana Sweets*, Dixie Poché admirably presents a panorama of Louisiana's best-known and most tempting "sweets" in their diverse richness. Cakes, pies, beignets, doughnuts, sweet breads, iced desserts, pralines, candy and fruit confections are just some of the delicious offerings featured on these pages along with the restaurants, bakeries, stores and other retail outlets where they may be found.

Supplementing the text is a wealth of vintage photographs, allowing the reader to step back in time and experience something of those beloved dining and entertainment places of yesteryear where many of the featured desserts and drinks gained wide renown.

FOREWORD

Louisiana Sweets is an invaluable resource not only for the cuisiniere and gourmand but also for anyone interested in Louisiana, southern and American culture and ethnic traditions. In its informative yet lively and easy-to-read format, *Louisiana Sweets* is a fitting tribute to the desserts and drinks that have made palates rejoice and Louisiana cuisine famous for nearly three centuries.

—BRIAN J. COSTELLO
Louisiana historian and author
New Roads, Louisiana

Acknowledgements

$\mathcal{L}$ouisiana's sweets are near and dear to my heart. What attracted me to this topic is more than the wonderfully delicious taste. Researching the origins of king cake, beignets and doberge cake proved eye-opening. Many Louisiana bakers have fine-tuned recipes from other lands by dressing up the dish to make it their own masterpiece. Memorable stories came from venues such as Leah's Pralines of New Orleans, the humble cottage business of Anna's Pies of Lake Charles, A-Bear's Café in Houma with its homemade bread pudding served in the midst of a Cajun music trio playing and the Easter basket memories evoked from the Gold Brick Egg of Elmer Chocolate of Ponchatoula.

What a delightful time I had sampling a treasure-trove of sweets here and there. Many thanks to Chris Jay at the Shreveport Bossier Convention and Tourist Bureau; historian Dr. Paul Leslie with Nicholls State University and Laurel Valley Plantation in Thibodaux; Joey Pierce with the Houma Visitors Center; photographer Travis Gauthier in Lafayette; Father Michael Russo with Our Lady of Fatima Catholic Church in Lafayette, who gave me an insider's view of the Sicilian tradition of St. Joseph's Day Altar; and Quincy Cheek, extension agent for Rapides and Grant Parishes, for her recommendations. Also thanks to Madeline R. DeBlieux with the Natchitoches Convention and Visitors Bureau; Tom Braniff with Domino Foods, Inc.; Scott Scheuermann with Elmer Chocolate; Dr. Laura Lyons McLemore with the LSU-Shreveport Archives & Special Collections of Noel Memorial Library; Melissa Smith and Michael Leathem of the

An ice cream cone promises a delightful way to cool off. *Photo by author.*

Louisiana State Museum; and Helen Thomas and Clifton Theriot with the Archives and Special Collections, Ellender Memorial Library of Nicholls State University.

I was excited to visit Georgia Morel at Morel's Restaurant in New Roads, an eatery that began life as a bait shop and was transformed into a great restaurant on False River. The Morels are truly dedicated to their community. When their restaurant was flooded in August 2016, everything had to be removed, cleaned, repaired and remodeled for a successful grand reopening a few months later.

Many recommendations were passed on to me during my hunt for wonderful dishes, eateries and old photographs. With some regret, I acknowledge that my taste buds were not able explore more, as Louisiana offers a flurry of sugary delights. I enjoyed every bit of my research at the luncheon counter. Lastly, merci beaucoup to my mother and aunts for their gift of memorable get-togethers and recipes.

Eat Dessert First

While growing up in a small community in southwest Louisiana, I shared many joyful Sunday afternoons with my Cajun cousins at my grandparents' farm located down a gravel road. At the homestead of Mom and Pop Douce Huval (*douce* is French for "sweet"), we mischievously poked around the pigeonniere, circled around pecan trees and played hide-and-go-seek near the cistern. During the summer, while the grownups sat on the front porch visiting, the kids clamored to be first in line to turn the hand crank of the ice cream maker. The cool prize was sloppy scoops of creamy homemade vanilla ice cream loaded with cherries. Laughing, talking about politics, rocking away the afternoon and bragging about old times were part of the entertainment. My uncle often began a joke in English but switched to French when he got to the punchline. The musicians in the family pulled out the accordion and fiddle and sang Cajun tunes.

Later, when I was too old to dress in mask and costume, I continued my Halloween tradition of dropping by Aunt Alice's house to enjoy her homemade praline or peanut butter fudge, which she handed out to all who visited her for trick or treat. My aunts and my mother, Gen, had their own sweet specialties. With the hint of baking drifting through open windows in our little country kitchen, it was no secret what Gen was up to on Saturday mornings—making cinnamon rolls from scratch. The rolls were yeast-based, prepared from a recipe that was passed to Gen from the school cafeteria ladies. She spent time kneading the dough, patiently allowing it to rise. It was rolled out flat in a rectangular shape, brushed with butter and

Louisiana's baked goods. *Courtesy of the Louisiana Department of Culture, Recreation and Tourism.*

sprinkled with a sugar-cinnamon mix. Once rolled into a log shape, it was cut in two-inch slices, nestled in round cake pans and baked as my sisters and I checked on the progress by peeking through the glass oven door. Once the fat rolls were declared ready and hot out of the oven, they were cooled on a rack followed by a drizzling of a light icing of powdered sugar and milk. The scent of cinnamon continues to remind me of home.

Gen also baked sweet dough pies using blackberries she picked in summertime and pecan pies during the winter, as we had plenty of pecan trees. Other family specialties were fig preserve cake made from home-grown figs in the backyard, pecan praline butter cake, tart a la bouille and a gussied-up coconut cake. Our summertime treats included snow cones, a slushy treat of frozen ice sweetened with flavored syrup.

Thriftiness was a common thread in Gen's desserts, as she grew up during the Great Depression. She often served gateau de sirop (syrup cake). Many southerners looked to the dark, flavorful sugarcane syrup as a sweetener, especially during difficult times. Imaginative homemakers used what they had on hand to create a worthy dessert despite limitations. They came up with the rich gateau de sirop using cane syrup as a sweetener and eggs from the chicken coop. As a kissing cousin to gingerbread, the syrup cake is a simple to bake, slightly sweet Cajun cake that does not have sugar or need frosting.

In the early 1900s, pear trees were plentiful on the Huval family property. My maternal great-grandmother, Malvina Naquin Huval, walked along the grove of trees in St. Martin Parish to collect the bounty of green pears. To make pear preserves, she peeled the skin from the pears, cut them into thin slices, tossed the lot into tall pots, added spices and cooked the batches on a wood-burning stove. This gift of nature in mismatched jars could be enjoyed year-round. By adding scoops of her preserves to regular butter cake batter, she created a memorable dessert: a moist pear preserve cake.

Other old-time desserts along the Bayou Teche included the Cajun Pig's Ear Pastry, or *oreilles de cochon*. This comes from the Louisiana tradition of family boucheries, or pig slaughters, in which every part of the pig was used to prepare dishes, such as boudin, crackling, sausage and bacon. But take heart, and do not jump to the wrong conclusion. The oreilles de cochon only bear a resemblance to the porky appendage. No part of the pig is actually used to create our Cajun version of a fritter. To prepare this fun treat, dough is formed into two-inch balls, flattened and shaped in a circle and rolled until thin. While deep-frying the treat, the cook uses a long fork to twist the dough in the shape of a pig's ear, followed by a quick drizzling of a heated mix of Steen's cane syrup and chopped pecans. In other areas, *langues de bouef*, or cow tongue pastries, can be deep fried and twisted in a similar way. Bread dough is rolled out and cut in three- by one-and-a-half-inch strips. Once fried until crispy, the special fritter is sprinkled with powdered sugar.

Why are memories so tied to food? I may not recall what Santa Claus delivered to us each Christmas, but I do remember that for special occasions, my mom prepared holiday treats like dates stuffed with a maraschino cherry cream cheese whip and topped with a pecan half. She also rustled up an addictive tidbit of a pecan roll cradled in marshmallow crème and toasted coconut. German chocolate cake with a pecan coconut icing offered a subtle chocolaty but delicious treat for Easter. Autumn evenings were spent rolling popcorn balls with syrup once the Jiffy Pop stove-top popping pan filled up with fresh popcorn. In honor of Gen's summer birthday, she pulled out cans of sliced pineapple and jars of cherries to make an outstanding pineapple upside-down cake that was drippingly delicious.

As my devotion to sweets continues, I reminisce about my introduction to my favorite showstopper of a dessert. The object of my affection was the fancy doberge cake with its shiny covering over six beautiful tiers. I took my good ol' sweet time (pun intended) to shamelessly savor the first luscious bite.

Pig's ear pastry known as oreilles de cochon. *Photo by author.*

Bedazzled by my visits to the old bakeshop, I studied the lineup of decadent delights. Parading past the showcase of gleaming chocolate éclairs, brownies and cream puffs, I mused over my choices. The seductive aroma of spices and baking drew me into a euphoric state. My head spun as some other delicacy captured my attention, whether it be cheesecake, petit fours, a sliver of the humble sweet potato cake or a dainty linzer cookie with jam filling. And that's why I say "Eat dessert first!"

> *Seize the moment. Remember all those women on the* Titanic
> *who waved off the dessert cart.*
> *—Erma Bombeck*

1

Louisiana's Sweet Heritage

*F*ollowing the path of Louisiana's culinary history leads you through a patchwork of foodways. When the Acadians were expelled from Nova Scotia to Louisiana as part of the "Grand Derangement," they learned about living off the land. In creating their own dishes, they were greatly influenced by other cultures—the Africans, Spanish, French, Germans, Italians and Native Americans. Although acclaimed for their style of preparing gumbo, boudin and crawfish dishes, Louisiana Cajuns and Creoles also enjoyed preparing desserts like praline, sweet dough pie and king cake. Other mouthwatering treats incorporated our natural resources of figs, fruit, berries and pecans. Why was Louisiana syrup cake (gateau de sirop) so popular during World War II? Why do we consider our bread pudding and pain perdu (lost bread or French toast) a secondhand treat? Perhaps it's because country cooks and later restaurant chefs repurposed what was available to them to dream up something spectacular.

DESSERT

The word *dessert* comes from the French *desservir*, which means "to clear the table." Trays of entrées and side dishes were cleared from the banquet serving area to make way for the final course. This stems from a medieval custom when the gentry class enjoyed sweetmeats and spiced wine to help

Cream puffs. *Courtesy of Gambino's Bakery.*

Serving dessert as a final course stems from a medieval custom. *Courtesy of Morel's Restaurant.*

their digestion following a feast. It evolved to something more elaborate, blossoming from preparing a few treats to assembling an extravagant display of fruit, cookies and cakes. The sweets were considered a luxury, allowing nobles to outdo one another in their overindulgence as a grand finale to an extraordinary affair.

Queen Sugar

We have celebrated the richness of sugar for many years. Is it any wonder that sugar has been tagged as white gold? Children in south Louisiana grew up chewing blocks of sugarcane for the juicy pulp inside. Considered a tropical grass that grows best (ten to twenty feet tall) in a warm, humid climate, sugarcane is a major source of commercial sugar.

Jesuit priests first brought sugarcane into south Louisiana from Santo Domingo in the mid-1700s. The variety of this early Creole cane was sweet and popular for chewing. Credit is given to planter Étienne de Boré for perfecting the process of sugar crystallization in 1795 at his plantation, the home of present-day Audubon Park in New Orleans. When de Boré successfully turned Creole cane into sugar, plantation owners took notice.

The shift from King Cotton to Queen Sugar as a prime agricultural commodity cannot be understated, as the importance of the sugar industry to Louisiana goes way back. Though sugar planters—primarily in southern Louisiana—recognized that there were greater risks by replacing cotton with sugar, greater rewards were foreseeable. Taking into account advancements in machinery such as the steam-powered mill, along with an increase in labor, Louisiana's sugar industry exploded with over 1,500 sugar-producing mills located in the state by 1840. It is estimated that 90 percent of the sugar produced in the United States during the antebellum period originated in Louisiana. Every aspect of producing sugar—whether planting, working the fields or harvesting—required a hands-on approach. So greatly did planters depend on African American slave labor that the slaves' hard work was considered the foundation of the success of sugar production. It is estimated that there were more than 300,000 slaves in Louisiana by 1860. Not only did slaves work in the fields, but they also played a critical role in running the plantation as skilled blacksmiths, carpenters, coppers, domestic cooks and nursemaids. Sugar cultivation has remained the major agricultural activity in the state since that time, continuing to play a crucial role by providing an annual economic impact of $3.5 billion.

According to the American Sugarcane League, 1.4 million tons of raw sugar are produced on more than 400,000 acres of land in twenty-two Louisiana parishes. Within these parishes, it is common to see sugarcane harvest activity run from October to January, though the actual planting of sugarcane normally takes place in September. Combine harvesters ramble through fields cutting standing cane stalks into pieces called billets, approximately 18 inches in length. Leaves at the top of the stalk are shredded and loaded on wagons and trailers and transported to a sugar mill for weighing, sampling and thorough washing before milling. The extracted juice is boiled to produce raw sugar and molasses. For miles around, the widespread aroma warns you that the process of crushing cane has begun. Raw sugar is then transported to a refinery, where it is cleansed to remove the molasses, allowing sugar crystals to form.

Iberia Parish, host of the annual fall Sugarcane Festival during the "sweetest time of the year" for over seventy-five years, is considered Louisiana's largest sugar-producing parish. Festival activities include a candy toss parade, crowning of royalty, an old-fashioned sugar cookery contest and a sugarcane judging contest. Sugarcane stalks are judged for weight and maturity during this unique contest for 4-H and Future Farmers of America (FFA) members.

AMERICA'S LARGEST SUGARCANE REFINERY

Sugar remains important to Louisiana's economy, as evidenced by the continued success of the Chalmette Sugar Refinery near New Orleans in Arabi. As America's largest cane-producing refinery, it was named in honor of the adjacent Chalmette Battlefield, where the Battle of New Orleans took place in 1815. Built from 1907 to 1909, the refinery was originally designed to process three million pounds of sugar daily. Though strictly a cane-producing plant—with the term "melt" used for what is produced—the refinery melts as much as 8.2 million pounds of sugar daily, of which 75 percent of the raw sugar received is from Louisiana's sugarcane fields.

The refinery is owned by the Florida Crystals Corporation and Florida Sugarcane Growers Coop under the umbrella of American Sugar Refining

Inc./Domino Sugar, a division of the American Sugar Refining Group (ASR). The construction of the refinery was quite an undertaking, including five million bricks produced on the north shore of Lake Pontchartrain. Originally, the buildings of the massive refinery in Arabi contained ten thousand windows. The first shipment of fifty-six thousand bags of raw sugar in 1909 arrived from Porto Padre, Cuba.

The refinery, as well as the entire sugar industry, experienced difficult times, such as hurricanes that hit New Orleans, a shortage of raw sugar in the 1920s and several fires that destroyed the docks where raw sugar was received. During World War II, there was a labor shortage of employees so as part of the Prisoner of War labor program, German soldiers who had been captured were transported to St. Bernard Parish and assigned to work in the plant for the duration of the war, though many chose to stay on when the war ended.

Domino Sugar caters to those with a sweet tooth by sponsoring an annual October Old Arabi Sugar Festival. Hosted by the Old Arabi Neighborhood Association, activities include a dessert competition and a doughnut eating contest. The St. Bernard Parish Tourism Commission is working with Domino to create an Old Arabi Sugar Museum.

Laurel Valley Sugar Plantation and Museum

Once one of Louisiana's leading sugar producers, Laurel Valley Sugar Plantation in Thibodaux is considered the largest surviving nineteenth- and twentieth-century sugar plantation complex left in the United States. First settled in 1790 by Acadian Etienne Boudreaux, the plantation remains a sugarcane farm encompassing 1,400 acres of working plantation fields. In 1834, Joseph W. Tucker bought the 600-acre Laurel Valley property as well as other nearby acreage along the Bayou Lafourche to develop sugarcane fields, thus expanding the plantation. The plantation sugar mill, constructed with 366,000 slave-made bricks, produced 1.5 million pounds of sugar with more than 130 slaves working sugar operations.

After the American Civil War, Laurel Valley Sugar Plantation changed hands a few times and was purchased at the end of the nineteenth century by partners Frank Barker Sr. and J. Wilson Lapine Sr., who had operated nearby Melodia Plantation. To increase productivity and save cane transportation expenses for sugar operations, a dummy railroad system was expanded. The efforts of modernization led to the processing of nearly four million pounds of sugar.

A variety of arts and crafts and local jams and honey are for sale in the plantation's restored country store and museum. On display are artifacts of early plantation life, such as photos, maps, models, tools and farm implements, giving insight into the history of sugar farming. The plantation property houses sixty original structures and has welcomed visitors to annual fall and spring festivals since 1984 that feature local arts and crafts and cultural demonstrations. Laurel Valley Sugar Plantation has been the setting for several movies, such as *A Lesson Before Dying*, *A Gathering of Old Men* and *The Butler*.

ANTEBELLUM SOUTHERN SWEET

Sally Lunn Bread

Sally Lunn Bread was a favored southern treat during the heyday of sugarcane production. The popularity of this slightly sweet, cake-like bread carried over throughout the American Civil War. As many staples were scarce or very expensive during these hard times, cooks used substitutes to prepare a treat for hungry soldiers. Cake ingredients like a pound of butter and a dozen eggs cost more than a pound of meat during this time. As a substitute for wheat flour, replacements of cornmeal, potatoes or rice flour could be used. In Louisiana, honey or syrup was often used as a sweetener in place of sugar. Was there really a Sally Lunn? One story goes that she was an English girl during the eighteenth century who first baked the yeast bread in a round cake pan. Another version attributes the name Sally Lunn to a French fille who prepared a tasty bread with a golden crust and light, pillowy slices that glow like moonlight, noting that *lune*, a variation of "lunn" is French for "moon."

Sally Lunn Bread (Quick Variation)
Courtesy of Author

2¼ cups all-purpose flour
3 teaspoons baking powder
½ teaspoon salt
1 teaspoon nutmeg

1 tablespoon cinnamon
1 cup buttermilk
½ cup (1 stick) butter, softened
½ cup sugar
2 tablespoons honey
1 large egg, beaten

Sift flour, baking powder, salt, nutmeg and cinnamon and place in large mixing bowl. Combine milk and softened butter and add to mixing bowl, blending until smooth. Add sugar to mix. Fold in honey and egg. Batter will be light brown; hand stir for 3 minutes until blended smoothly. Preheat oven to 375 degrees and bake 30 to 35 minutes, until crust is golden. Remove from oven, let cool for 5 minutes and remove from pan. Cut bread into slices. Serve with jam or jelly.

EARLY BAKERIES

Today's much-loved bakery may have evolved from sweetshops and confectioneries of Europe. While colonists carried over their love of sweets and traditional recipes, they also brought over seeds and cuttings for fruits and vegetables to begin their new life. During America's colonial period, the bakery focused on producing bread at a time when loaves were priced by weight when sold to customers, who enjoyed bread at every meal. The lead baker and his apprentice started the laborious job of baking before dawn by heating up the brick oven. Bins of the essential ingredients of flour, yeast and salt were sorted. Hours were spent hand-kneading the dough to allow time for rising. Long-handled wooden bakers' peels resembling paddles were used to place the bread loaves in and remove from the oven. Gradually, bakeries began offering additional goods, such as pastries and cakes, incorporating seasonal fruits and berries. Molasses or honey was added as a sweetener, as sugar was expensive. So dear was sugar that it was sold in cones that were locked in sugar boxes.

The inspirational story of one early Louisiana bakery shows how a business dedicated to sweets affected lives in an amazing way by showing compassion to the less fortunate.

In the early 1800s, five-year-old Margaret Gaffney and her family crossed the Atlantic Ocean, emigrating from Ireland to America. Her father, a farmer, looked to America for opportunity by finding work in Baltimore. Tragedy struck when four years later, both of her parents and a younger sister died during a yellow fever epidemic. At age nine, with no formal training (indeed she never learned to read or write), a homeless and penniless Margaret began domestic service until marriage in her twenties to Charles Haughery. After the couple moved to New Orleans, tragedy struck twofold by the passing of Charles and soon after by their daughter.

Margaret remained in New Orleans, taking in laundry and doing ironing to support herself. Located in her neighborhood was the Poydras Orphan Asylum run by the Sisters of Charity. Margaret's donation of time and money to the orphans kicked off her fifty-year involvement in community charitable work.

To provide money and fresh milk to the orphans, Margaret purchased two cows and a milk cart, eventually becoming owner of a dairy with a milking herd of forty cows. During this time, she also opened a humble stand along the New Orleans levees, selling her freshly baked bread and coffee to sailors at the docks.

With her growing nest egg, she bought the first steam bakery in the South in 1859, naming it Margaret's Steam & Mechanical Bakery. Combining efforts with forty employees, she baked cakes, breads, crackers and other goods, with profits directed to the orphanage, schools and a Catholic church. During the Civil War, Margaret faced many challenges, one being how to get the necessary supplies she needed for her baking. Despite the circumstances of wartime, she continued to feed soldiers on both sides—Confederate and Union alike.

As the "Bread Lady of New Orleans," Margaret Haughery dedicated her efforts to helping others and was beloved as a friend of orphans. Upon her death in 1882, she left her estate—valued then at $500,000—to the Sisters of Charity for orphans as well as to other New Orleans orphanages. A statue was erected in her honor in Margaret Park in New Orleans, adjacent to the original orphanage and St. Teresa of Avila Church. Called the *Margaret* statue, only the second in the nation portraying a woman, it depicts the humble Irish woman in her later years holding a small child.

INTRODUCTION OF CANE SYRUP

There's an old adage "When life gives you lemons, make lemonade," alluding to using some creativity to turn a challenge into something positive. This advice applied to a dire situation in which a southwest Louisiana farmer faced the dilemma of fields of a frozen sugarcane crop, which he turned into a crop of a different sort.

In 1910, C.S. Steen of Abbeville foresaw a devastating financial loss before him because of his frozen sugarcane. To prevent financial ruin, he studied how to salvage his crop. By investing in a small mill through a local hardware store and using open kettles, he produced barrels of syrup in which pure sugarcane juice was evaporated and cooked to create caramelized cane syrup. Five generations later, the Steens continue to use the original recipe and steam equipment to make their 100 percent pure cane syrup.

For pouring on hot buttermilk biscuits, French bread, pancakes and even boudin links, cane syrup became Louisiana's treasured replacement to the North's maple syrup. Many recipes, whether sweet or savory, have been improvised to make use of this buttery nectar. Since the early 1900s, the yellow can of Steen's syrup has been a handy pantry staple for use in baking pecan pies, gingerbread men, gateau de sirop (syrup cake) and spice cookies.

Ginger Crisps
Courtesy of Steen's 100% Pure Cane Syrup

¾ cup shortening
¾ cup sugar
½ cup Steen's Pure Cane Syrup
1 egg
1½ teaspoons baking soda
1 teaspoon cinnamon
½ teaspoon ginger
¼ teaspoon salt
2¼ cups all-purpose flour, sifted
⅛ teaspoon ground cloves

Cream together shortening and sugar until light and fluffy. Add syrup and egg; mix well. Sift in remaining ingredients; mix thoroughly. Place in freezer 1 hour or chill in refrigerator 2 hours. Form into approximately 1-inch balls; roll in granulated sugar. Bake on greased baking sheets at 375 degrees for 10 to 12 minutes. Makes 4 dozen cookies.

BAKING CONTEST

During World War II, families experienced shortages and rationing of food items, with happy days resuming in America at war's end in 1945. As soldiers returned home to their families, a surge of prosperity was welcomed as well. Housewives who had once scrimped to prepare dinners during the war visited the grocery store with a new freedom and could now afford to purchase sugar and butter for home baking.

New homes were built with help from the GI Bill, and once set up, they had to be fitted with modern appliances like the electric refrigerator, which made food preservation simpler. Many homemakers who had joined the workforce during wartime continued to work. They longed for meals, including desserts, that could be jiffy-ready. The trend of cooking from scratch to packaged foods, TV dinners and cake mixes was introduced as "almost" home cooking but partnered with convenience to save time.

Gearing up for the first Pillsbury Bake-Off® launched in 1949. *Courtesy of General Mills Archives.*

To celebrate Pillsbury's eightieth birthday, a national competition to show off the culinary skills of American women was launched in 1949. The first Pillsbury Bake-Off® Contest was held at the Waldorf Astoria in New York City. Thousands of entries were submitted, with the first contest's winning entry receiving the grand prize of $50,000, awarded by First Lady Eleanor Roosevelt. The winning recipe—a sweet nut roll bread named "No-Knead Water-Rising Twists"—used a unique rising method of wrapping the dough in a tea towel and submerging it in warm water. Each decade of the Pillsbury Bake-Off® reflected changes in consumer trends that homemakers followed. In the 1950s, the biggest category for entries was "scratch cake." Also during that timeframe, a junior division was implemented, drawing in a younger crowd. In the 1960s, mixes and refrigerated dough became qualifying products; in the 1970s, one of the grand prize–winning recipes was a bar cookie with only seven ingredients—reflecting the busy schedules homemakers faced between raising children and running a house. During the 1980s, a microwave category was added.

Why These Dishes Are Timeless

As thrilled as southern bakers were by the convenience of shortcuts through cake mixes, they were also smart enough to keep a stronghold of much-loved family recipes, often written on an index card. Special notes may have been added, like "use brown sugar instead of white sugar" or "good to add a cup of pecans." And when penned in Grandma's handwriting, these generational recipes and the dishes that were prepared go hand-in-hand with joyful memories. Maybe the sight and lingering aroma of these cakes, cookies and pastries lead to recollections of baking and hosting holidays. And that's why these special dishes remain timeless.

Happy Birthday

Celebrating milestones with a birthday cake, whether chocolaty devil's food or heavenly angel food, is over eight hundred years old. In Ancient Greece, candles atop cakes represented the light of life and symbolized the glow of moonlight to honor Artemis, goddess of the moon. Blowing out candles while

Jazz musician Louis Armstrong cutting a gigantic birthday cake at his seventieth birthday in 1971. *Courtesy of the New Orleans Jazz Club Collections of the Louisiana State Museum.*

making a wish was a sign of upcoming good fortune. The celebratory cake was later tied to a medieval German tradition of Kinderfest, when birthday cakes were prepared for children. As a time-honored custom to honor someone special, birthday cakes tagged with a party became fashionable in America after the Civil War.

2

Beignets, Doughnuts and Calas Cakes

BEIGNETS

Café Du Monde
800 Decatur Street
New Orleans

Louisiana's state doughnut, the beignet, is named for the French term for fried dough or fritter. This famous New Orleans specialty square is a mixture of flour, milk, water and yeast dough that is deep fried, served hot and dusted lavishly with powdered sugar. Two differing stories explain how the beignet traveled to Louisiana. In one version, the French Acadians who were exiled from Canada brought many dishes and unique foodways with them to Louisiana, including the beignet. A second story credits the Ursuline nuns of France for bringing the recipe to Louisiana in 1727.

An entertaining spot to find beignets is the world-famous Café Du Monde in the French Market of New Orleans, established in 1862. There is a general rule to follow while sharing a platter of beignets. Just as you wouldn't wear a white shirt when eating boiled crawfish in Louisiana, you shouldn't wear black when biting into a beignet—the powdered sugar will fly everywhere. It's amazing to watch the frying process, as little pillows of dough scramble in hot oil in a race to the top, for that's when you know the beignets are done, as well as by their golden color.

World-famous Café Du Monde in New Orleans, 1939. *Courtesy of the Collections of the Louisiana State Museum.*

As one of the most photographed restaurants in America, Café Du Monde (*monde* means "world" in French) bestows a perfect setting for a "come as you are" gathering, as you may sit next to a glam wedding party or a sleepy-eyed visitor after an evening on Bourbon Street. *Time* magazine put together an interactive map of "The Most Instagrammed Places of America," and in Louisiana, the top site is Café Du Monde. People are lured in twenty-four hours a day, seven days a week, though the café is closed on Christmas. To avoid long lines, it is suggested that you stroll in before sunrise to enjoy the sweet treats served in orders of three.

The atmosphere of this coffee shop includes the happy sounds of calliope playing on the steamboats on the Mississippi River and an amazing view overlooking Jackson Square and St. Louis Cathedral. An inviting companion to the beignet is café au lait. This Louisiana potion is a regional blend of coffee and chicory. Once brewed, hot milk is added half and half to the cup. Chicory, the root of the endive plant, is added to dark-roasted coffee to smooth out the bitter taste.

CALAS CAKES

The Old Coffee Pot Restaurant
714 St. Peter Street
New Orleans

A kissing cousin to the breakfast beignet is the calas cake. Like many Louisiana dishes, it came from a frugal tradition of transforming leftovers into a delicious treat. Many Louisiana dishes, such as gumbo and jambalaya, feature rice, an important southern crop after the Civil War. So the calas cake, a dense rice fritter, was well suited to its debut over one hundred years ago.

To prepare these fritters, leftover cooked rice is transformed into a pudding by adding eggs, sugar, cinnamon and nutmeg. The mixture is rolled into a small flattened cake, lightly battered and dropped in the frying pan. Once lightly fried—the crunchy cake bears a resemblance to a hush puppy—the calas cake can be dusted with powdered sugar or drizzled with syrup.

This crisp around the edges dish was carried over to Louisiana by slaves from the rice-growing areas of Africa. The name "calas" is said to have come from an African Nupe word *kara*, meaning "fried cake." Chants of "Belle calas! Tout chaud!" announcing that the beautiful cakes were hot and ready to eat could be heard throughout the French Quarter of New Orleans.

With covered baskets filled with delicacies balanced on their heads, African American women sold the homemade treats to parishioners after Sunday mass services. In Louisiana, the Code Noir mandated that slaves were given Sundays off, allowing them opportunity to sell their calas cakes and other wares as a way to raise money to buy their freedom. It became a popular street food, though the lovely beignet has surpassed it in popularity.

If you spend your evening in New Orleans drinking hurricanes at Pat O'Brien's Bar on St. Peter Street, you'll note the Old Coffee Pot Restaurant two doors down. Known for its great breakfast dishes, the Old Coffee Pot is one of the few places that include calas cakes on the menu. Opened in 1894, the restaurant was formerly a house with classic New Orleans décor—a nice outdoor courtyard as well as an inside dining area, a spiral staircase and scattering of wrought-iron accents. It's purported to be haunted, but when you're in New Orleans, you expect many of your dining and sleeping quarters to have ghosts hanging around. If your waitress calls you "baby" or "sugah," she's simply sending a little southern hospitality your way.

DOUGHNUTS

Southern Maid Donuts
3505 Hearne Avenue
Shreveport

The glorious puff of gooey deliciousness with a hole in the middle known as the doughnut had early beginnings in Europe. It may have evolved from *olie bollen*, a fried treat brought over to America by early Dutch settlers. When bakers began braiding the dough, the name of the pastry evolved to "dough knots." First becoming a hit with American soldiers during World War I, many were introduced to these fried rings by female Salvation Army volunteers called "Lassies." As a way to conserve supplies, these snappy treats were fried in batches—seven at a time—in soldiers' helmets. These snacks were distributed by the Red Cross to soldiers on the battlefield during war, although the volunteers during World War II were nicknamed "Donut Dollies." As the war progressed to victory, GIs were sometimes corralled to huge tent cities to enjoy a million cups of coffee and a half million doughnuts every day.

In 1934, the doughnut became the talk of the town when it was billed as the "Hit Food of the Century of Progress" during the Chicago World's Fair. Hundreds of doughnuts were churned out by machines to feed to visitors. That same year, before actor Clark Gable played rogue Rhett Butler in the epic *Gone with the Wind*, he portrayed a newspaper reporter in a screwball comedy. In *It Happened One Night*, Gable introduced Claudette Colbert to the fine art of dunking a doughnut in a steaming cup of coffee, thus securing more fans of the delightful treat.

The Salvation Army created National Doughnut Day on the first Friday in June 1938 to honor the many volunteers who served doughnuts to soldiers during the Great War. The day also tied in with a fundraiser in Chicago to help the needy during the Great Depression.

Those pleasant puffs covered with sugary glaze are not just served for breakfast. Every day at 4:00 p.m., you can find a line at Southern Maid Donuts, a historic doughnut shop in Shreveport. Hot doughnuts have been served in this shoebox-sized setting since 1937, when the Hargrove family started the business following the Great Depression.

You can spot the bright neon sign of Southern Maid Donuts for miles around. The retro shop features a "Cavalcade of Stars" wall of photos

Doughnuts served to soldiers during World War I. *Courtesy of the Salvation Army USA.*

dedicated to the stars of *Louisiana Hayride*, the national radio program broadcast from Shreveport that featured musicians such as Hank Williams, Johnny Cash, Faron Young and Johnny Horton. As Southern Maid Donuts was one of the sponsors during the program, many of these stars were regular customers.

Before he was "nothin' but a hound dog," Elvis Presley started performing with the *Louisiana Hayride* at age nineteen. The only product he ever promoted commercially was Southern Maid Donuts, in 1954. This was likely when Elvis began his love affair with jelly doughnuts. The radio jingle he sang proclaimed, "You can get them piping hot after 4:00 p.m.; you can get them piping hot. Southern Maid Donuts hits the spot, you can get them piping hot after 4:00 p.m."

Elvis Presley performing at the Louisiana Hayride in Shreveport in 1954. *Courtesy of the LSU-Shreveport Archives and Special Collections.*

Rickey Meche's Donut King
402 Guilbeau Road
Lafayette

This iconic shop with a fifty-year history started with founder Ewell Meche (Rickey's father) while he was delivering newspapers to an existing doughnut shop on the north side of Lafayette. The owner encouraged Meche to buy his shop, which Rickey now owns. Doughnut shops are fast-paced, following a routine of early mornings and lots of hands-on tasks. Meche's gives two stories to answer the age-old mystery of why there is a hole in the middle of the doughnut: they fry better and slipping a finger through the hole makes it easier for kids to handle.

Aside from the lovely doughnut, another specialty of Meche's is the three-braided king cake, fried just like a doughnut rather than baked. It's decorated in the Mardi Gras colors of purple, green and gold and jam-packed with delicious fillings—chocolate is one of the favorites. The shop atmosphere is reminiscent of a diner, with red and white accessories and a motto of "Making Your Day a Little Sweeter." It's a comfy place where kids breeze in wearing their pajamas. Meche's also prepares banana nut loaves in eight different flavors. Their busiest times are Mardi Gras,

Nascar Sunday and Super Bowl Sunday. The success to making great doughnuts is by following the recipe precisely and keeping the right timing and temperature of frying, mixing, bundling and proofing. The steps to this sequence are a sight to behold as the doughnut-cutting machine works with thin layers of dough gliding through while big round cuts and a smaller cut for the doughnut holes are made. But Meche's always has a backup plan when the machine is ornery, as the team is experienced in hand-cutting with amazing speed if necessary.

Ray's Bakery
971 East Laurel Avenue
Hwy 190 East
Eunice

Glaze the doughnuts, roll out the cookie dough and get the elephant-shaped cookie cutters ready. Time to take out the loaves of French bread hot out of the oven. Cupcakes are ready to be frosted. It takes a whole heap to run a bakery.

Since 1959, Ray's Bakery has been putting smiles on faces with its "everything's made from scratch" sweets. Ray Oncale started his bakery in 1957 in the small town of Church Point, eventually relocating down the road to Eunice, self-proclaimed Prairie Cajun Country Capital. With business acumen in his background, Ray had helped many family members launch bakeries in Crowley, Lake Charles and Opelousas. Family recipes in hand for cakes, cookies and doughnuts are what convinced Ray to establish his own sweet shop along with brother-in-law Richard Allen. Ray's is now owned by son Steve Oncale, with family members at the mixer, rolling tables and ovens. While still a frequent stop for visitors coming through, Ray's is located on Highway 190, once the major east–west thoroughfare through southwest Louisiana. A baker's life means an early start, and Sundays are the busiest. Customers wait in line for the favorites of puffy doughnuts and butter bead cookies. Specials in 1959 for Ray's grand opening were thirty-nine-cent pies and dollar cakes.

3
Cakes

"Let them eat cake!" These legendary words, attributed to Marie Antoinette, bride of France's King Louis XVI, in the late 1700s, were spoken to her hungry French subjects during a bread shortage. The cake, or *brioche* as it was called in France, was more of a sweet bread tinged with honey with little resemblance to today's baked confection of numerous varieties, layers and configurations. Credit France with developing the dish to a lighter density, gradually leading to the showpiece we worship today.

One important circumstance that has helped American bakers through the years was the introduction in 1929 to store shelves of the first

A cake lover's paradise at the Bordelonville Homemade Cake Festival. *Photo by author.*

commercial cake mix: Dud's Gingerbread Mix. The mix contained the standard ingredients of flour, sugar, baking soda and baking powder along with spices and powdered molasses. With many homemakers excited about this shortcut to preparing a dessert, the company soon introduced other flavors. By the 1950s, two hundred manufacturers were turning out cake mixes, such as Pillsbury, General Mills and Betty Crocker. Early cake mix boxes included bonus recipes for frosting, keeping the cake homemade, though faster to prepare.

BORDELONVILLE HOMEMADE CAKE FESTIVAL (APRIL)

Bordelonville, Louisiana

Countless festivals and church fairs entertain Louisiana folks and visitors throughout the year. Not to be outdone, the little community of Bordelonville, which sits peacefully along Bayou des Glaises in Avoyelles Parish, was contemplating ideas for a unique festival to raise funds for the volunteer fire department's community center. Bordelonville is a close-knit community that already hosts a *cochon de lait* (pig roast) in the fall. Along with accolades from visitors about the pork dishes, there were rave reviews about the homemade cakes that graced dining tables. Chocolate, pineapple, coconut, caramel, you name it—the bakers in the area make sure that a variety of the best selection of cakes is prepared. And that's how the Bordelonville Homemade Cake Festival was launched. Hosted for the first time in April 2016, the festival displayed more than 250 cakes made by volunteers sold as a whole cake or by the slice, with the promise that visitors will go home happy by sampling the array of delights. In addition, the festival provided Cajun snacks like cracklings, jambalaya, crawfish pistolettes and pulled pork sandwiches. Entertainment included bingo, a dance, a decorated cake contest and cake walks, in which lucky contestants won a cake. A few miles away was another celebration: the 100th anniversary of the Sarto Old Iron Bridge, one of the few remaining steel swing truss bridges in Louisiana.

Following are two favorite recipes from the festival. The first is a recipe for the filling for caramel pecan cakes. It comes from the cookbook *Cooking on the Bayou*, published by the ladies of St. Peter's Altar Society (available by contacting St. Peter Catholic Church in Bordelonville at (318) 997-2151).

Caramel Pecan Filling
Courtesy of Faye Mayeux

½ cup margarine
1 ½ cups light brown sugar
⅓ cup whole milk
2½ cups powdered sugar
3 to 4 cups ground pecans
¼ teaspoon almond extract
1 pinch of salt

Melt margarine. Add brown sugar and cook 2 minutes while stirring. Add milk and bring to a full boil. Cool. Make sure mixture is cool enough so powdered sugar won't be lumpy when mixing. Add powdered sugar, ground pecans, extract and salt. Stir. If too thick, add more milk until smooth enough to spread between cake layers.

Pineapple Sour Cream Cake
Courtesy of Mrs. James "Dardene" Armand

1 box butter cake mix
1 can crushed pineapple
½ cup sugar
⅓ cup cornstarch
2 tablespoons butter
2 tablespoons lemon juice
8 ounces (1 package) sour cream
Buttercream icing (recipe of your choice)

Mix cake according to package directions. Divide batter into 4 pans. Bake and cool. Cook pineapple, sugar, cornstarch, butter and lemon juice until thick. Let cool. Stir in sour cream and spread mixture between layers, reserving approximately ¼ cup. Ice the cake with buttercream icing, leaving a circle in the center to the top bare. Place reserved pineapple filling in the bare spot on the cake. Refrigerate before slicing.

Black Forest Cake

From the land of cuckoo clocks, Gothic churches and waterfalls comes the dream cake called *Schwarzwalder Kirsch*, Black Forest cherry torte in German. Four layers of chocolate sponge cake and cherries make this rich dessert memorable. Traditional costumes of the region in the colors of black like chocolate flakes, white like cream and red pompoms like cherries may have influenced the name. Frosted with whipped cream and covered with chocolate shavings, the cake is decorated with cherries. It may be generously flavored with Kirschwasser (cherry schnapps).

The name Black Forest draws up picturesque images of a Bavarian wonderland of trees swathed with snow, gentle slopes along mountains and crystal lakes. While working at a German café in 1915, pastry chef Josef Keller invented the elaborate Black Forest cake, a union of chocolate and cherries.

Julie Anne's Bakery & Café
825 Kings Highway
Shreveport

One regional takeoff on this German delight is the Black Forest meringue cake. Shreveport's chef/restaurateur Shorty Lenard created such a cake fifty years ago. Although he died in 2003, his gift of a one-of-a-kind dessert lives on in a few bakeries in Shreveport. Julie Anne's Bakery prepares a similar cake using almond flavoring, though without cherries on top. It's a sophisticated meringue treat of stacked layers with German chocolate filling that melts in your mouth. Preparation takes many hours, with lots of eggs to mix, plus some time to freeze the wonderful cake.

Renato Majstorovic, his wife, Anela, and their children came to Shreveport in 1997 from Bosnia after civil unrest forced them to leave their country. Friends suggested that they move to America and choose a small town to make adjusting to American life easier. Anela worked under the original bakery owner Julie Anne Nelson, who opened this charming little sweet shop in 1992, while Renato worked at a local restaurant. Their American Dream came true when an amazing offer was made to the Majstorovics to buy the bakery, including the recipes of all of the sweets. Mornings begin at 3:00 a.m. in the bakeshop to allow time to make lots of goods, including bread for

Black Forest Cake, the German delight. *Courtesy of the Shreveport Convention & Visitors Bureau.*

their lunch and dinner sandwiches, including a national favorite of Bosnia, a sandwich called cevapcici. It's a comfy place to pop in to enjoy hot pastries.

To introduce their native dishes to Louisiana, the bakers prepare baklava during the Christmas season. A many-layered pastry, baklava is moistened with melted butter before baking and soaked in syrup. Filling consists of nuts such as walnuts or almonds. Regional variations may include adding cinnamon to the nuts or rosewater or honey to the syrup.

Once the Christmas holidays are over, then the phenomenon of carnival season takes hold with Julie Anne's king cakes. Over ten thousand of the gold, green and purple cakes are carted off by customers during Mardi Gras season. A king cake is similar to a coffee cake, though usually shaped as an oval ring. The custom suggests that a small plastic baby is inserted in the king cake, and the individual who gets the baby must buy the next cake. With a variety of twenty flavors to choose from, choices include praline, lemon and cream and brownies and cream. A Black Forest version is dreamy, with chocolate, cream cheese and cherries. King cakes are available year-round and can be seasonally decorated for Valentine's Day, Easter or other special occasions.

Middendorf's Restaurant
30160 Highway 51 South
Akers

A remarkable view of Lake Maurepas—along with a repertoire of boiled and fried seafood—has pulled folks to this out-of-the-way restaurant for over seventy-five years. New Orleanians enjoy the easy drive across the Bonnet Carré Spillway to enjoy Middendorf's specialty of thin fried catfish. It's a casual eatery with several corners for dining, including a back deck right on the water with an adjacent playground of sand for the kids to enjoy. The eatery enjoys a Hawaiian shirt kind of atmosphere, as though you were on summer hiatus listening to the sound of seagulls, enjoying the breeze off the water or taking a sunset walk on the pier. Make your holidays even better by catching a glimpse of a pelican convention, as Louisiana's state birds gather at Middendorf's to bring in the new year.

Louis Middendorf was a traveling salesman in Houston when he lost his job during the 1929 stock market crash. This led to an unexpected opportunity for the family to move to the fishing village of Manchac in Tangipahoa Parish, where his wife's family lived. Louis and his wife, Josie,

Middendorf's Restaurant on Lake Maurepas, established 1934. *Courtesy of Middendorf's.*

opened a café in 1934, with Josie assigned as chief cook using family recipes and Louis tending the bar and greeting customers. Their sideline job was running the Manchac Post Office.

Revamping of the restaurant through the years has included modernizing the kitchen and adding a large covered deck for waterfront dining. Royalty has dined here, including Prince Albert of Monaco, as well as another kind of royalty—Eli, Peyton and the Manning family. Now owned by Horst and Karen Pfiefer, the restaurant hosts a special Oktoberfest every October and November and offers German dishes such as wiener schnitzel and sauerbraten and desserts like Black Forest cake and apple strudel for a nice finishing touch.

RUSSIAN CAKE

Haydel's Bakery
4037 Jefferson Highway
New Orleans

The story of Haydel's Bakery covers fateful twists, turns and dogged perseverance. In 1959, when budding entrepreneur Lloyd Haydel took over an existing walkup doughnut shop in New Orleans called Sunny Flake Donut Shop, his original intention had nothing to do with doughnuts. Rather, his plans were to turn the former fruit stand and doughnut shop into the area's first trampoline center. Unfortunately, this business venture did not take off. Not one to give up, Lloyd recognized that customers were enthusiastic about the quality of the doughnuts he served. So instead of continuing with trampolines, he found himself running a successful doughnut shop, renaming it Haydel's Sunny Flake Bakery. Now it is run by the third generation of the Haydel family. In the late 1980s, David Jr. began working in the doughnut shop after school when he was only eleven years old.

In 1964, Hurricane Betsy changed the face of the doughnut shop by leveling it. Upon rebuilding the shop, the family simplified the name, calling it Haydel's Bakery. The range of baked goods was expanded beyond hot doughnuts to include wedding cakes, king cakes, pastries and more.

By looking to New Orleans' history in the realm of cakes, the Haydels brought back by popular demand an 1872 dessert, the Russian rum cake, which was invented to welcome Grand Duke Alexis to New Orleans during the first Rex Carnival Parade. This patchy cake uses leftover trimmings and cutaways of cakes. It's another frugal way that bakers prepare a special dessert by not wasting baked scraps. The Haydel version is an amazing combination of chunks of gold, devil's food and almond cake, all mixed with raspberry jelly, rum flavor and a hint of anise. The unusual combination is layered into a special cake pan. The process that makes this cake memorable is compressing the crumbly jumble overnight. Homemade buttercream icing is slathered on in the morning, transforming the lovely recycled sweet into a Russian cake.

Haydel's Bakery has a claim to fame: it set a 2010 Guinness World Record for the largest king cake. Haydel's teamed up with the New Orleans Saints football team to create two giant braided king cakes that wrapped around the Mercedes-Benz Superdome. The special event served as a fundraiser to benefit cancer research for the Susan G. Komen Foundation. The finished cakes—which took bakers three days to bake and over six hours to assemble—weighed 8,688 pounds and were 5,300 feet long. Ingredients included 4,000 pounds of Danish flour, 428 dozen eggs, 299 pounds of cinnamon sugar, 286 pounds of yeast and the finishing touch of 331 pounds of black and gold sprinkles, the colors of New Orleans Saints.

The bakers appealed to the Cajun population by coming up with a Christmas Cajun Kringle® in 1989. Haydel's version is a flaky, hand-rolled buttery pastry stuffed with a praline filling, topped with caramel icing and decorated with pecan bits. This sweet, nutty holiday treat resembles the ring shape of a king cake but has a different taste and texture. The Cajun Kringle comes complete with a story about a little baker, Alfonse, and his adventure with a big gator while traveling on the bayou in his pirogue.

OOEY-GOOEY CAKE

Buck & Johnny's
100 Berard Street
Breaux Bridge

This is a tale about second chances.

First, there's the ooey-gooey cake. The name pretty much tells all about this finger-licking dessert born in the 1930s in St. Louis, Missouri. While half-heartedly following a recipe, a German American baker bungled the dish by reversing the quantity of butter, adding more than the recipe called for. And presto, he came up with a sugary, sticky jumble that grew into a bestseller. Using cream cheese, lots of butter and powdered sugar in the mix, you can't go wrong with Buck & Johnny's version of the rich, jiggly in the middle ooey-gooey cake. And yet there other tempting desserts on the tray. Chef Tony's bread pudding is warm, creamy and luscious. Other sweets include rock slide brownie, red velvet cake and cannolis.

Secondly, at one time the top spot for fixing flat tires and doing tune-ups in Breaux Bridge, Buck & Johnny's is housed in the former Domingue Motors, built in the early 1920s. The garage closed in 1985 and was abandoned for many years, becoming an eyesore. In a commitment to revitalize the town, David Buck and business partner, the late Johnny Raymond, had the vision to dramatically transform the former garage into a center of an antique marketplace, glassed-in private events venue and a restaurant seating 240. Today, the eatery is owned by David Buck, Coatney Raymond and Heather Buck Indest.

Opened in 2010, Buck & Johnny's has a nostalgic style. Old buckets and auto accessories are used as plant holders. Oil cans have been repurposed as light fixtures. There's a bench mounted with a truck tailgate and Texaco signs displayed throughout to carry the auto theme. The restaurant's open second-floor loft overlooks the woodsy Filling Station Bar. It's a sit-down,

Buck & Johnny's, the "Eclectic Italian with a Cajun flair" eatery, was once a garage in downtown Breaux Bridge. *Courtesy of Buck & Johnny's.*

family-oriented pad, considered an eclectic Italian restaurant with a Cajun flair. Chef Tony Savoy prepares entrees ranging from pasta and pizza to gumbo and salads.

Live music is regular entertainment on weeknights. So when Coatney Raymond, a former hospital administrator who now runs this sassy eatery, had the opportunity to continue the tradition of hosting the "World Famous Zydeco Breakfast" in downtown Breaux Bridge, she jumped at the opportunity. Drawing visitors in to the French-speaking town of Breaux Bridge was a wonderful step to promote the Crawfish Capital of the World.

Zydeco is a jumping up, excitable kind of music with French Creole beginnings that often include the accordion and scrub board. An early influence was Clifton Chenier through his 1965 song "Zydeco Sont Pas Sale," meaning "snap beans not salty." Tables are pulled aside to make room for the two hundred eager dancers who show up at Buck & Johnny's by 8:00 a.m. on Saturday mornings to two-step to the lively music. Mimosas and Bloody Marys are on tap as well as some unique regional breakfast dishes. The Ti Na Na is a six-inch Cajun boudin pizza with red sauce, pepper jack cheese, spicy boudin, pork skins and—to add a little sweet—Steen's Cane Syrup.

FIG PRESERVE CAKE

A symbol of peace and prosperity, the fig was brought to America in the early 1500s by Spanish Franciscan missionaries who traveled to California in their quest to establish Catholic missions. Varieties of the juicy fig range in color from purple black to almost white with shapes of round to oval. The fig tree is popular in Louisiana because it thrives and looks neat in landscaping schemes with its big, somewhat rounded leaves and bulbs of juiciness hanging seductively throughout the tree. Doesn't it seem that the best figs are always way at the top of the tree, only within reach when you are standing on a ladder?

Fresh figs are unfussy. They're easy to handle because they are the right size to pop into your mouth. Since figs perish quickly, care must be taken to prepare them in jams or preserves. Many folks recall going to Maw-Maw's house during the summer to harvest buckets of plump figs. Luckily, this is followed by time spent in country kitchens with the sweet scent of fig preserves cooking on the stove with lots of sugar. Fig preserve cake, like many other dishes, was well-loved among resourceful homemakers, as they could use what they had on hand. A pint of fig preserves added to a batter makes a succulent cake, good enough for company.

Krewe Chic-a-la-Pie Mardi Gras Kaplan

In treasuring the history of Mardi Gras and hospitality, one unique Mardi Gras *krewe* (club) shared an old recipe for the fig preserve cake, a popular dessert of *les vieux temps* ("old times") along the bayou.

Louisiana is well known for its celebration of Mardi Gras (Fat Tuesday), the last blast before the solemn Lenten season begins. Widespread revelry is enjoyed, way beyond the ritzy glam of New Orleans carnivals. One krewe deep in Cajun Country, Kaplan's Krewe Chic-a-la-Pie is famous because it was originally an all-women's group, begun in 1952. It was formed as a way of preserving the customs of a French-Acadian Mardi Gras, stemming from a tradition in the late 1800s near what is today the town of Kaplan (an area once known as Cossinade) in Vermilion Parish. Activities included the Courir du Mardi Gras in which a masked group led by Le Capitaine stopped at various houses begging for donations of chickens, pigs or money to prepare a huge feast on Mardi Gras night. In exchange for these goods, the revelers entertained the neighborhood by singing, dancing, performing acrobatics or playing musical instruments.

The name of the krewe comes from a whimsical Mardi Gras rhyme: "Mardi Gras, Mardi Gras, Chic-a-la-Pie, Give me your nose, And I'll make you a pie." Some say that *chic-a-la-pie* is slang for chewing on a piece of straw.

During early days, krewe members wearing funny masks and ridiculous dress as they rode around in trucks to visit family friends entertained kids with their mischief. In 1956, festivities grew to include a parade with floats made from simple materials like chicken feathers, dyed stockings and Spanish moss for decoration. The symbol of flowing sheaths of rice, representing Vermilion Parish's main crop, was freely displayed. Queen Jambalaya and King Gumbo ruled over a fanciful ball and other carnival events. That same year, Krewe Chic-a-la-Pie began contributing to a charitable organization that continues to this day. In recent years, the parade and street dancing promote the French heritage of the area and attract over fifteen thousand visitors.

Fig Preserve Cake
Courtesy of Krewe Chic-a-la-Pie

2 tablespoons sugar
1 egg
1 teaspoon vanilla
½ teaspoon baking soda
½ teaspoon cinnamon
½ teaspoon nutmeg
½ teaspoon salt
1 teaspoon baking powder
1 pint mashed figs
1 cup plus 3 tablespoons flour
½ cup cooking oil

This is a simple cake with no frosting necessary. In a bowl, add sugar and egg and beat well. Add vanilla, baking soda, cinnamon, nutmeg, salt, baking powder and figs and mash well. Add flour and oil and stir until well blended. Preheat oven to 300 degrees. Pour batter into a lightly greased round cake or loaf pan and bake until well browned (about 30 minutes). Stick a toothpick in the center to see if it comes out clean. Let cool before serving.

Doberge Cake

In a city that thrives on celebrations, New Orleans boasts its own birthday cake, the extravagant doberge cake. Doberge is a multilayered round sponge or butter cake filled with a kettle-cooked custard and finished with poured fondant icing, typically of chocolate or lemon.

The towering cake of six to eight thin layers evolved from the *dobos torte,* a European sensation named after its creator, Hungarian baker Jozsef Dobos. He debuted his novelty cake at the National General Exhibition in Budapest in 1885. It received much attention, garnering high praise from Queen Elisabeth and Emperor Franz Joseph, who sampled the experimental dessert, which was universally proclaimed a great success.

Gambino's Bakery
4821 Veterans Memorial Boulevard
Metairie
Additional locations in Lafayette, Baton Rouge, Gretna

The story of this old-world cake, the doberge, continued to New Orleans when homemaker Beulah Ledner faced hardship during the Great Depression. Remembering the basics of German baking from her mother, Beulah created a takeoff from the Hungarian dobos torte. She improvised the classic recipe by replacing the buttercream filling with a lighter custard and finished the cake using a thin layer of fondant icing instead of the original dobos torte's caramel topping. Beulah's final customized treat was an eight-layer yellow cake with homemade chocolate custard sandwiched between each layer and a final pouring of two types of chocolate frosting. In changing the name to *doberge* she added a French influence to reflect the tie to New Orleans. Through the makeshift bakery and tearoom she opened in her own home, the doberge cake was introduced to the neighborhood for sampling. Residents unabashedly adored the sensational sweet.

In 1946, she temporarily retired due to her failing health as well as the difficulties of rationing, which limited sugar and other staples. It was at this time that Joe Gambino bought the retail shop Beulah Ledner Bakery along with its signature recipes. In 1949, the local bakery was refreshed and reopened as Joe Gambino's Bakery, gradually simplified to Gambino's Bakery, which now has four Louisiana locations. Gambino's Bakery reigns as a top spot for delicious baked goods, though a slice of the glossy-topped doberge cake continues to reign supreme among loyal followers. Using the 1946 recipe, Gambino's expert bakers take four hours to prepare the famous buttermilk cake with six delicate layers, which are baked individually. It's a dream come true for those indecisive customers who want it all, because Gambino's prepares a half lemon and half chocolate doberge as well as caramel or strawberry.

Aside from the doberge cake, Gambino's has a long list of specialty desserts—éclairs, cookies, petit fours and its hallmark Mardi Gras delight, the king cake. To this day, Gambino's continues the baking tradition of Beulah Ledner and Joe Gambino of keeping things pure and delicious by making all of its products from scratch on a daily basis.

KING CAKE

Think like royalty when you come across the enchanting king cake decorated in colors of green, gold and purple and bedecked with Mardi Gras beads. Known by many names, Twelfth Night Cake or king cake is big business—coffee room talk and Twitter conversations revolve around who bakes the best. Not only is the cake richly dressed and delicious, but it also comes with a prize. Is the taste of the king cake more like a doughnut or a cinnamon roll? Is it filled with cream cheese? Is the top covered with colored sugar or icing?

During carnival season, which begins on Twelfth Night or the Epiphany, bakeries and grocery stores abound with their own variety of the lip-smacking king cake. Most often it is designed as a three-braided coffee cake, shaped in an oval ring. Alas, the test-tasting ends on Ash Wednesday, which is recognized as the beginning of the Lenten season, and for the most part, the indulgence is curbed. Once slices of the cake are cut and shared, a frantic search begins for the slice with the small plastic baby representing baby Jesus. The taster with the baby in his cake slice has the honor of buying the king cake for the following week for everyone to share.

Twelfth Night honors the wise men who visited the manger in Bethlehem at the time of Jesus's birth. During medieval times, part of the celebration of Twelfth Night included serving a cake in which a bean, coin or even something as extravagant as a ring was hidden. Traditions of a king cake associated with choosing a king or queen were later carried over to New

Orleans carnival balls. The lucky guest who found the token in his dainty morsel of cake was named lord of the evening's entertainment. This honor also entitled him to command guests to do his bidding—as well as to choose a lady as his queen to accompany him on a musical promenade. Scotland's version of the king cake is known as the "black bun," although it resembles a dark holiday fruitcake and is spiced with whiskey or brandy. In Spain and Mexico, the king cake is known as *rosca de reyes*.

Poupart Bakery
1902 W. Pinhook Road
Lafayette

In the early 1960s, Louisiana welcomed François Poupart, who had worked as a pastry chef in Paris, and he fell in love with the small-town charm of Lafayette. Sharing his French language with the locals also endeared him to the area. In opening his own *patisserie* (pastry shop) and *boulangerie* (bakery), he brought in the best of the old country cuisine to Lafayette. François Poupart still enjoys making an assortment of baked goods—his famous François Frenchies dinner rolls, brioche made with lots of butter and eggs, buttery croissants and no fat–no sugar baguettes. As he hand-kneads the dough and rolls out the bubbles, he jokingly recognizes that "bread is always the boss," meaning that you have to compromise when working with the temperamental dough.

Poupart's has glitzy French specialties like fruit tarts, éclairs, macarons, praline and chocolate ganache, cheesecake, the summertime Chantilly cake of blueberries and strawberries and rum cake.

Staying true to their French roots, François and his son Patrick continue to prepare the true French king cake or *galette de rois*. This golden delight has a layer of thick homemade almond cream similar to marzipan sandwiched between two round layers of light, flaky pastry. Poupart's is one of the few bakeries that offers this original king cake in honor of the French celebration of Epiphany called *Fete des Rois*, or "Festival of the King," a custom since the fourteenth century.

A visit to Poupart's takes in all of your senses. There's the aroma of fresh goods as well as the view of the bustling of bakers shelving hot-out-of-the-oven breads along with the ongoing scurry of pastries being filled, stuffed and decorated. A bounty of colorful jars of Poupart's own pickled green beans, beets and chow-chow are lined up on the shelf. International sweets are displayed, like Italy's tiramisu and cannolis, Greece's baklava and France's crème brûlée. Another masterpiece is the six-layered dobash cake, as this is how Poupart's calls its famous cake, though labeled doberge cake by others. Poupart's offers its dobash cake as chocolate covered or half lemon/half chocolate. Poupart's has a second location in downtown Lafayette, both preparing soup, sandwiches, salads and quiche for lunch in addition to worldly sweets.

Crystal Weddings Bakery
110 Mimosa Place
Lafayette

Mary Boudreaux of Crystal Weddings Bakery has over thirty years of experience in baking and preparing a range of cakes, from king cakes to elaborate bride and groom cakes. Baking birthday cakes for children in her home kitchen was how she began. With a passion for baking and a desire to learn more, Mary, whose baking skills are self-taught, invested in a Wilton decorating kit. Now she is baking wedding cakes for some of these same customers who enjoyed her birthday cakes when they were children. Her daughter, Crystal, who followed in her footsteps, briefly relocated to New York for culinary training in the finer arts of decorating cakes, especially

Treasure-trove of king cakes during carnival season. *Photo by author.*

glamorous wedding cakes. A few years ago, the Crystal Weddings Bakery was featured on the TLC show *Outrageous Kid Parties* along with the fourteen-layer, life-size alligator cake that the bakery created for a *Swamp People* theme.

Recognizing the popularity of Lafayette's carnival season, Mary and Crystal ventured into the king cake business, offering over twenty different flavors in a miniature size, which serves two to four, all the way up to large, which serves twenty to twenty-five.

The most rewarding part of preparing the king cake is the finale—the light drizzling of icing. The whole process from start to tasting takes several hours of patience—letting the dough rise, kneading, cutting, proofing and rolling the dough out to make strips that are braided and connected to form a round king cake. If the cake will be graced with a fruit filling, the strips are rolled down and flattened and a flavoring is slathered on. Forty-five cakes are baked in the oven at one time, with a baking time of less than twenty minutes. After competing in a regional contest, Crystal Weddings Bakery has been honored as "Best King Cake" in Acadiana.

Quebedeaux's Boudin & Cracklins
3710 S. MacArthur Drive
Alexandria

Their "kicked up" version of the king cake sells like crazy, featuring a tinge of sweet. But in true Cajun style, there is a somewhat shocking addition of a special ingredient that gets tongues wagging, as this king cake is stuffed with the meaty Louisiana sausage called boudin.

Quebedeaux's (pronounced kib-a-dough) prepares its specialty Mardi Gras king cake by laying out a strip of bread dough that has been punched a few times as their way of kneading. A link of homemade boudin is cut open, and the rice and sausage mixture is removed from the casing, scooped and spread over the dough. The ends of the dough are joined to form an oval shape. Once the bread is baked in the oven to a golden tint, a slightly caramelized praline sauce of butter and sugar cooked in an iron pot is drizzled on the cake. Although praline sauce normally includes pecans, this one-of-a-kind king cake is topped with pork crackling bits to add crunchiness. Homemade colored sugars tinted in purple, green and gold are sprinkled over the baked bread as a zany finish. This unexpected creation of sweet and spicy takes three hours to prepare, with everything homemade. Although especially popular during carnival season, the boudin king cake is available year-round by special order.

This specialty dessert was a family effort cleverly inspired by Chef John Valenzuela from Lafourche Parish. His wife, Leslie Quebedeaux, is from the Pecaniere area of St. Landry Parish. Her siblings share a culinary interest, as one owns a series of boudin shops, one owns a spice business and one owns a sausage company. A few years ago, the family challenge focused on how to come up with a showstopper kind of king cake to satisfy culinary cravings. After a few tryouts in a test kitchen, the Quebedeaux team was thrilled with the unique king cake. In time, it was back to the chopping block to create yet another new flavor by introducing a jalapeño boudin king cake using jalapeño powder blended with cream cheese for the stuffing.

By working under Chef Paul Prudhomme in New Orleans and at Enola Prudhomme's Cajun Café in Carencro, Louisiana, Chef John learned a lot about layering flavors. He blends a Cajun influence with a touch of New Orleans style, incorporating some great smothering (étouffée) techniques in his savory dishes of pork roast, red beans and rice, gumbo and seafood for his daily plate lunches. Quebedeaux also make its own seasoning available at the swamp-style chic shop, along with boudin balls and tamales. In October 2016, Chef Valenzuela was one of eight Louisiana chefs participating in a special food event in Charleston, South Carolina, called Louisiana in the Lowcountry Restaurant Night, which introduced southerners to the Bayou State's special cuisine.

La Boulangerie
4600 Magazine Street
New Orleans

Cochon Butcher
930 Tchoupitoulas Street
New Orleans

Louisiana cooks do not rest on their laurels. With so many opportunities for experimenting with ingredients and new combinations, chefs magically dream up more creations. Take the king cake designed by French bakery and neighborhood café La Boulangerie, which provides handcrafted breads and pastries for local locations of the Link Restaurant Group, including Peche, Herbsaint and Cochon Restaurants. The Elvis King Cake honors Elvis Presley's favorite over-the-top peanut butter sandwich. The fantasy cake is filled with fresh bananas, peanut butter and diced house-cured bacon and topped with toasted marshmallow cream. Rather than a plastic baby, a tiny pink piglet is hidden in one of the cake slices—a cute touch from Cochon's Restaurant, as *cochon* is French for "pig." *USA Today* proclaimed this crazy sweet as one of the "Best Mardi Gras King Cakes for 2016."

CUPCAKES

Isn't the cupcake just a smaller version of a fancy cake? As a palm-sized delight, it is served in its own crimped liner and dressed up with a fancy swirl of frosting. The cupcake likely evolved as a downsized version of the pound cake, taking its name from the cup, a common measuring tool used while preparing a basic cake recipe of one cup of butter, two cups of sugar, three cups of flour, four cups of eggs and so on. In 1927, Hostess introduced its version of this favored dessert as a crème-filled snack cake. Originally a devil's food cake with signature white squiggly lines decorating the top, the Hostess® Cupcake originally sold for a nickel.

Sophi P Cakes
3211 Johnston Street
Lafayette

The Sophi P recipe for sweet success paired Jennifer Melancon's passion and pastry skills with her husband Dustin's marketing savvy and restaurant experience. Throw in some out-of-the-box business thinking and a name that fit their fun and funky shop. Sophi P is Lafayette's first cupcakery, though there is actually no person or mascot named Sophi P, as the unique name stands for "sophisticated punk."

When Jennifer was growing up in Lafayette, her vision was to one day run her own bakery. Rather than trying her kitchen skills with an Easy-Bake Oven as a tot, she began with a full-sized oven, happy to prepare

Strawberry Fields 4-Ever cupcake.
Courtesy of Sophi P Cakes.

her own birthday cakes while a teen. Her mother encouraged her to enter a regional cooking contest, which further inspired her to reach for her dream.

Years later, she and Dustin brainstormed on what type of sweetshop to undertake. In 2010, they renovated a former ice cream shop from the 1960s by setting up home mixers and ovens. Instead of running a full-service bakery, they chose to craft made-to-order cakes. Years of old-school training and experience as a pastry chef gave Jennifer the necessary skills, though she also enjoyed incorporating her own ideas at the baking table.

In late 2009, TV's Food Network introduced the reality show *Cupcake Wars*, ushering in a craze for the cute, pint-sized cakes. "Who had the superior cupcake?" was the focus, as teams competed in taste and presentation.

Lady luck stepped in on the timing, as Sophi P was laying out its red carpet for cupcakes by focusing on producing these favored sweets. Originally, the ovens were baking eight dozen at a time—though with upgrades they have progressed to twenty dozen cupcakes at a time.

When scheming up new flavors, Dustin agrees that their team members improvise by trying out favorite ingredients they enjoy eating, like pistachios or amaretto. They also consider regional flavors with the Southern Belle, a sassy sweet potato cake with a spicy praline butter cream accented with toasted pecans. A favorite is the S'Mores Delight, which magically blends chocolate cake, graham cracker buttercream and a toasted jumbo marshmallow. To prepare their pecan pie cupcake, the bakers dedicate forty minutes of slow-cooking on the stove to prepare pecan pie filling to blend with a yellow cake and top with cream cheese icing and cinnamon sugar pie crust crumble. There's a tribute to the Fab 4 of the Beatles with Strawberry Fields 4-Ever, and Mardi Gras time features a king cake cupcake. *USA Today* recognized Sophi P's regal treat as one of the best Mardi Gras king cakes for 2016.

The Melancons agree that while baking, you have to pay attention to precise measurements and consistency of techniques and ingredients. Sometimes, despite their best efforts, cupcakes may come out lopsided, though just as tasty. If they do, the tops are sliced off and used to create a playful take on the flying saucer–shaped UFO's, ultimate flavorable objects, in which two cupcake tops are sandwiched and filled with rich frosting. Some of the cupcake recipes include throwing in a little pinch of Cajun seasoning to mix sweet and spicy. Many of their ideas can be traced back to the tastes of grandma's kitchen.

A few other yummy options have been introduced, such as baklava cheesecake; custom shot-glass desserts; cutie pies, which are mini chocolate mousse pies; puff pastry sweets; and their savory creation—boudin quiche. Also popular are skyscraper towers of elegant cupcakes served at weddings with a piece de resistance cake top decorated with pearls or fancy twirls.

Recognition was given to the "hang loose" cupcakery in 2016 when it was recognized as a Small Business of the Week for serving as a great example for all aspiring female entrepreneurs during October National Women's Small Business Month, which celebrates more than 9.8 million small businesses owned by women in the United States.

4

Candy and Praline

CANDIED AND CARAMEL APPLES

Candied and caramel apples may remind you of childhood romps through the big top and carnivals. With good reason, these delights became a favorite in concession stands on circus grounds.

A New Jersey candy maker is credited with combining the right amount of red cinnamon candy and apples to invent the red candy apple in 1908. With a surplus of cinnamon candy on hand for Christmas, he experimented by dipping an apple into the melted candy mix, placing the dressed-up apples in his show window and selling them for a nickel apiece. A new craze unexpectedly took off, making the candied apple popular at candy shops and carnivals along the Jersey shore.

In the 1950s, Kraft food employee Dan Walker found a way to use up the abundance of caramel squares from Halloween. By melting the caramel and dipping the apples by hand into the creamy blend, he discovered another tasty treat. Ten years later, an automated caramel apple machine was invented to simplify the process of making this snappy delight.

The Chocolate Crocodile
460 Boardwalk Boulevard
Bossier City

Though considered traditional autumn treats, candy-coated and caramel apples are available year-round at the Chocolate Crocodile, located at the boardwalk along the Red River in Bossier City. There's a lot of dipping by hand—to the count of 160 apples three times a day.

Peel away another layer of this popular shop with its variety of wacky apples, opened in 2005 by Jim and Cyndi Rogon. Big enough to share, the scrumptious Monstrous Candy Apple fits the name, as this juicy two-and-a-half pound Granny Smith apple is covered in homemade caramel, dipped in milk chocolate and smothered with crunchy nuts. The Granny Smith is the apple of choice because it's crisp and tart.

A sense of nostalgia draws fans to this fun-loving spot, which has a host of unexpected add-ons for its apples, such as white chocolate, nuts, candy bars or English toffee. The Apple Pie Apple is simply an apple dipped in caramel and covered with white confection and rolled in brown sugar. Other homemade candies, including fudge, divinity, pretzels dipped in chocolate, marshmallow on a stick dipped in chocolate, cake balls, bark and peanut brittle, are primed in glass cases, ready for tasting.

This sweet shop attracts school tours, as it celebrates chocolate every day. On-site demos prove that everything tastes better covered in gooey chocolate—even carrots, grapes and mushrooms. Be forewarned about a cool display of a chocolate-covered alligator. Although you will find alligator dishes on dining menus in Louisiana, this shop's chocolate croc is pure confection.

The Chocolate Crocodile has two other locations in the South: Huntsville, Alabama, and Cypress, Texas. The busiest times are Valentine's Day and Christmas, although National Caramel Apple Day on October 31 is a great day to celebrate a revved-up treat during a hobgoblin holiday.

PRALINES

Let's honor the most recognized bite-size treat of the South. In its simplest form, the praline is a bonbon of sugar and butter cooked slowly until the luscious blend caramelizes. It tastes best when pecans are added for crunchiness. Once the blend reaches the right stage, it is dropped by spoonful on a cooling table. This cherished Creole candy of various sizes and shapes may be pronounced "praw-leens" in some regions and "pray-leens" in others.

The namesake of the praline is the Duke of Plessis-Praslin, whose chef invented sugar-coated almonds as a means to cure indigestion. Although no proof exists that it actually alleviated the duke's ailment, the French candy certainly had a big following during the early seventeenth century because it was sweet, used few ingredients and was easy to prepare.

America's love affair with the sweet delight began with a New Orleans businessman's chance sampling of a praline of almonds during a visit to Paris. In tasting the praline, he developed a sweet tooth passion for the simple candy. Upon his return home, he challenged his cook to duplicate the effort, though almonds were substituted with Louisiana's plentiful pecans. Another version of how the precious confection ended up in Louisiana relates to the Ursuline nuns' trek to New Orleans from France in 1727. Praline making was part of the culinary education the nuns introduced to the casket girls, who were young women sent over from France at the request of Louisiana governor Jean-Baptiste Le Moyne Bienville to marry into the colony. With the growing popularity of pralines by the mid-1800s, Creole women called *pralinieres* cooked and sold batches of these tasty delights throughout the French Quarter of the thriving port city of New Orleans.

Leah's Pralines
714 St. Louis Street
New Orleans

Situated in a city that prides itself on pleasing le monde with culinary choices, Leah's Pralines in the French Quarter is one of the oldest family-owned praline shops. It was first known as Cooks Confections, which opened under Cecil Cook in 1933 on Rampart Street, later moving to St. Louis Street. It is actually believed to have been launched even earlier, as it was listed in the 1933 New Orleans' City Directory at the original location of 521 South Rampart Street.

Fashion model Leah Johnson knew next to nothing about making candy, but when she chanced upon Cook's Confection coming up for sale in 1944,

Fashion model Leah Johnson acquired a New Orleans praline shop in 1944. *Courtesy of Leah's Pralines.*

she and her husband, a financial consultant, jumped on the opportunity. They bought the candy-making business, which was located in an ideal spot, directly across from the famous Antoine's Restaurant.

Although a new entrepreneur, Leah had charming ways to attract customers and work the counter with a pronounced poise, charm and graciousness. She and her husband, O.K. Johnson, lived in an apartment above the shop, always near to the business. As the glamorous storefront face of the confections, Leah managed the business, which originally offered only three products—frosted pecans, pralines and pecan brittle—although Creole fudge and pecan nougat logs were later added.

During the 1980s, Leah's niece Elna Stokes took charge of the business, preserving the same recipes, which have not changed much in seventy years. Peak exposure to Leah's Pralines came in 1984 when New Orleans hosted the World's Fair.

Today, Elna's daughter Suzie Stokes runs the show, filling up candy jars in a quaint atmosphere of homemade goodness carried over from Aunt Leah. Suzie grew up helping out in the store while her mother, who was a schoolteacher, owned the praline shop. Suzie often rode a streetcar to school, returning to the shop to do homework in between being pulled into packaging or working the counter. Upon graduating from Loyola, Suzie moved to New York and began a career as a graphic designer. Suzie's brother Kenny also dedicated many years of working in the praline shop. He currently lives in Boston and is credited with creating the bacon pecan brittle recipe, another sweet treat that Leah's is famous for. The bacon pecan brittle is distinctively sweet and savory with bits of bacon blended in with thin brittle.

Upon Suzie's homecoming to New Orleans, she returned to school, this time earning a culinary degree from Delgado College. She gained experience as a pastry cook in New Orleans restaurants, eventually returning to her family's candy-making business.

Pecan brittle. *Courtesy of Leah's Pralines.*

Whether making small or large batches, the shop's two candy makers continually stir the wooden paddle to cook pralines in the original copper kettle until the sugary syrup reaches the right stage. Additional products have been added since Leah's time in the shop. One of the other new products considered the belle of the ball is Cajun Mud—a funny name for layers of rich chocolate, caramel and pecans. Other choices include chocolate fudge and Leah's praline sauce, which is great for pouring over ice cream. The shop's indulgent repertoire of pralines (creamy, traditional, rum and chocolate) are good choices to serve as party favors. Fresh batches of pralines are made daily–to the tune of five hundred—even more during the busy holiday season.

In 2014, Martha Stewart recognized Leah's Pralines as a pioneer in the candy-making business by naming the entrepreneur an "American Made Food" finalist for creating beautiful, useful products and changing the way we eat, shop and work.

Elmer Chocolate
401 North Fifth Street
Ponchatoula

As a food of the gods, chocolate was originally served as a somewhat bitter beverage to the elite class. Cocoa, which is used to produce chocolate, originated with the Aztecs, who cultivated the seeds of the tropical *Theobroma cacao* tree. According to the National Confectioners Association, it is estimated that 70 percent of cocoa currently comes from the 1.5 million specialty cocoa farms in West Africa. Approximately three million tons of cocoa beans are turned into chocolate products annually.

Zing goes the arrow as Cupid makes plans for Valentine's Day, looking to Elmer Chocolate in Ponchatoula for the hallmark gift of candy. As the second-largest manufacturer of heart-shaped boxes of candy in North America, Elmer's produces forty to fifty million boxes annually of specialty bonbons.

Elmer Chocolate is one of the oldest family-owned chocolate companies in America. The company is a true Louisiana institution of sweets, having started in New Orleans in 1855, a time when the Crescent City was the largest city in the South as well as the financial center for the Mississippi Valley. Many startup businesses offered services to both residents and visitors by providing good meals and sweet treats. It was during this antebellum time that German immigrant and pastry chef Christopher Henry Miller, along with son-in-law Augustus Elmer, started the Miller Candy Company. In 1914, the Elmer family changed the name to Elmer Candy Corporation.

In 1963, the company changed hands when Roy Nelson purchased it and encouraged his son to join the operation, which had moved to the little town of Ponchatoula, north of New Orleans. After research taste-tasting, the company found its niche by concentrating on seasonal chocolates rather

The Gold Brick Egg was introduced in 1936 as a one-ounce nugget of chocolate and pecan, selling for a nickel. *Courtesy of Elmer Chocolate.*

than everyday candy and snacks. Currently run by the third generation of the Nelson family, Elmer Chocolate has chocolate galore, including caramel, strawberry crème and chocolate fudge. Melt-in-your-mouth delights are prepared for Christmas, Valentine's Day and Easter with a tagline of "Celebrate with Chocolate."

Most families in the Deep South look forward to an Easter basket of sweet eggs as they did during their childhoods. Elmer's popular Heavenly Hash® Eggs, from a 1920s New Orleans department store recipe, combine double-rich milk chocolate with puffy marshmallow and fresh roasted almonds. Elmer's Gold Brick Eggs were introduced in 1936 as a one-ounce nugget of chocolate and pecan. Selling for a nickel, the bar was wrapped in foil reminiscent of the gold bricks stacked in the vaults of the U.S. Mint. Customers enjoyed a sense of richness when they hurriedly unwrapped the delightful chocolate. The popularity of this "million dollar candy bar" goes one step further with the availability of Gold Brick topping (golden Louisiana pecan pieces in creamy milk chocolate that forms a hard candy shell) poured over ice cream for a special treat.

The company recently completed a $40 million expansion of its state-of-the art manufacturing facility in Ponchatoula, where the plant produces four million pieces of chocolate candy daily.

5
Cold Treats

SNOWBALLS

Snowballs or snow cones? What better way to celebrate Louisiana's summertime meltdown than with a chilly treat. Aficionados recognize that snow cones are made with crunchy, crushed ice while snowballs are the refined prima donna of a fluffy-textured shaved ice. Both are soaked in a variety of colorful sugary syrups of iridescent shades. It's a cheap and quick way to get cool as the heat bounces off the sidewalk. Sampling the bubblegum flavor guarantees that your tongue will turn a nice hue of blue for a few hours, helping you to forget how hot it is outside.

Hansen's Sno-Bliz
4801 Tchoupitoulas Street
New Orleans

New Orleans was the site for one of the first electric snowball machines, which produced shaved, snow-like ice, in the 1930s. Machinist and tinkerer Ernest Hansen developed the mechanism, and along with his wife, Mary, he opened a small shop in 1939, selling the first snowballs for a penny apiece. Now run by granddaughter Ashley Hansen, the

Hansen's Sno-Bliz began courting customers in 1939. *Courtesy of the Louisiana Department of Culture, Recreation and Tourism.*

hangout churns out timely flavors of satsuma, ginger cayenne, cream of coffee and Bananas Foster. Hansen's continues to offer old flavors as well, though fancy toppings like whipped cream and marshmallow fluff are fun additions. New Orleans offers many memorable experiences, and visiting Hansen's is another classic one. Upon entering the flimsy screen door entrance to this simple cinderblock stand, veteran customers instruct novices to "follow the yellow brick road," a painted yellow line that helps them line up to place orders at the counter. This route allows customers to make their choices. The maze guides you amid the grinding sound of the ice shaver and the dousing of cones with in-house syrups to keep folks happy and refreshed. If you feel rushed about holding up the line, go with the traditional strawberry or wedding cake flavor. The cream variations have an added bonus, sort of like slurping down a snowball with a scoop of ice cream mixed in. In 2014, the James Beard Foundation recognized Hansen's as an "American Classic," honoring this long-running establishment that represents the best of American regional food.

Babe's Snowballs
916 S. Main Street
St. Martinville

Located on the main drag in historic St. Martinville, Babe's has served snowballs since 1949 in a building as colorful as the rainbow snowballs that are served. Ed "Babe" Robertson barely has time to sit down, so busy is he taking orders, scooping up fresh ice and over-stuffing foam cups among the kaleidoscope of neatly organized syrup bottles lined up on the counter. Customers aged toddler to one-hundred-plus are challenged to select which flavors to try in anticipation of a spoonful of fun. The bestseller is strawberry, although the variety includes piña colada, wedding cake, grape and lots more. Busy times are noon and midafternoon, when school is letting out, as this out-of-the-ordinary roadside stand is an easy walk and bike ride from neighborhoods. The menu is simple: snowballs and potato chips, that's all. The eye-catching metal snowball sculpture hanging above the stand was built by Babe when he was eight years old and supervised by his grandfather. Babe's paycheck for helping was fifteen cents, which he used to buy a movie ticket. This led to Babe's career of making the hand-scraped icy treats. Catering is a sideline; he recently prepared five hundred snowballs for a local school.

BAKED ALASKA

Baked Alaska is a tricky mix of hot and cold. In simple terms, it's an ice cream cake that undergoes an elaborate meltdown. A sponge cake is topped with a brick of ice cream and ingeniously covered with an uncooked meringue, frozen until showtime. Just before serving, there's a quick pop into a hot oven until the meringue is lightly browned. The amazing part of the whole production is that the ice cream keeps its cool and does not melt because it is insulated by the meringue blanket.

A variety of tales about the dish's creation abound, though clearly it was not first prepared in its namesake, "The Last Frontier" state of Alaska. In 1802, President Thomas Jefferson served his White House guests an early version of baked Alaska, simply ice cream within a hot flaky baked shell.

One story tells us that in the mid-nineteenth century, a Chinese delegation visited Paris, and the head cook of the group shared with

Louisiana's mayhaw berries. *Courtesy of Travis Callahan.*

Silken chocolate pecan tart. *Courtesy of the National Pecan Shellers Association.*

Above: St. Joseph Altar, a Sicilian tradition of thanksgiving. *Courtesy of Our Lady of Fatima Catholic Church.*

Left: Blueberry pie. *Courtesy of the U.S. Highbush Blueberry Council.*

Candied apples may remind you of the big top. *Photo by author.*

Pecan pie, a southern classic. *Courtesy of the Louisiana Department of Culture, Recreation and Tourism.*

Left: Slice of blueberry coffee cake. *Courtesy of the U.S. Highbush Council.*

Below: Peach pound cake. *Courtesy of Del Monte Foods, Inc.*

Above: Delicious little pies at the Kitchen Shop in Grand Coteau. *Photo by author.*

Right: Tart and custardy key lime pie. *Courtesy of the Florida Keys Visitors Bureau.*

Strawberry cake. *Courtesy of Ambrosia Bakery.*

Sweet tater pie tart. *Courtesy of the Louisiana Sweet Potato Commission.*

Upside down pear pie. *Courtesy of Del Monte Foods, Inc.*

An old-fashioned sweetshop, Champagne's Bakery, established in 1888. *Photo by author.*

Right: Flaming Bananas Foster is a showstopper. *Courtesy of Brennan's Restaurant.*

Below: Elvis King Cake with a touch of bananas, peanut butter and crumbly bacon. *Courtesy of La Boulangerie.*

Left: Vintage trade card of an essential baking ingredient: corn starch. From the New York Public Library.

Below: Baked Alaska, a tricky mix of hot and cold. *Courtesy of Antoine's Restaurant.*

Left: Fabulous Russian cake. *Courtesy of Haydel's Bakery.*

Below: Louisiana's state doughnut, the beignet. *Courtesy of the Louisiana Department of Culture, Recreation and Tourism.*

Cook's
Southern
Confections
OLD NEW ORLEANS

CREOLE
CANDIES AND
DELICACIES
•
MADE FROM
THE RECIPE
OF AN OLD
LOUISIANA
FAMILY

COOK'S CONFECTIONS
ACROSS FROM ANTOINE'S
714 ST. LOUIS ST.
NEW ORLEANS, LA.

Above: Cook's Southern Confections ad. *Courtesy of Leah's Pralines.*

Right: America has had a love affair with the praline since the early 1700s. *Courtesy of Leah's Pralines.*

Above: Watermelon and apple pie macarons at Sucre in New Orleans. *Courtesy of @hanafoto.*

Left: Macaron cookies during carnival season at Sucre in New Orleans. *Courtesy of @hanafoto.*

Tray of sweets. *Courtesy of Gambino's Bakery.*

The many layers of the doberge cake. *Courtesy of Gambino's Bakery.*

Coffee service
set with dessert.
*Courtesy of Morel's
Restaurant*

Roi de gateaux, old-fashioned French king cake. *Courtesy of Travis Gauthier and Poupart's Bakery.*

Bread pudding is no wallflower dessert. *Courtesy of Elizabeth's Restaurant.*

Bananas Foster pain perdu. *Courtesy of Elizabeth's Restaurant.*

Louisiana has a colorful heritage of sweet delights. *Photo by Darren Hebert.*

French chefs the technique of baking ginger-vanilla ice cream within a pastry crust. It was known as *Omelette Norvegienne* or "Norwegian omelet." Yet another tale says that the dish was prepared in New York City's Delmonico's Restaurant in 1867 and named in honor of the United States' acquisition of the territory of Alaska. Originally called "Alaska Florida" in reference to the unusual hot and cold aspects of the dish, it evolved to baked Alaska.

Antoine's
713 St. Louis Street
New Orleans

Considered America's oldest family-run restaurant, Antoine's in New Orleans' French Quarter has given its guests memorable culinary creations like Oysters Rockefeller, a dish of baked oysters with spinach. It was named in honor of oil tycoon John E. Rockefeller because of the richness of the sauce. A famous Antoine's brew is café brulot ("burnt coffee") a boozy after-dinner cocktail/coffee drink. The special effects of this nightcap include a flaming finale as the drink is lit up at the table. Café brulot was introduced in 1890 and became especially popular during Prohibition as a means of concealing liquor.

This landmark restaurant of French-Creole cuisine has fine dining in fourteen showcase rooms. Because of Antoine's historic ties to Mardi Gras, many of the rooms bear the names of carnival krewes and are filled with photos and memorabilia of past royalty. During its remarkable 175 years in business—through the American Civil War, Great Depression, World War I and II and Hurricane Katrina—Antoine's has hosted numerous noteworthy guests, such as Franklin D. Roosevelt, Bob Hope and Bing Crosby, Pope John Paul II and the Duke and Duchess of Windsor, during their 1950 visit to Mardi Gras.

Antoine's is owned and operated by fifth-generation relatives of founder Antoine Alciatore. An eighteen-year-old immigrant from Marseille, France, he spent two years in New York City looking for wealth and prosperity. Luckily, he chanced a trip to New Orleans, which shared his French language, and established a humble boardinghouse and restaurant. The business eventually expanded and moved one block away to the elegant Antoine's Restaurant in 1840. This was the year that New Orleans experienced a business growth as the third-largest city and second-largest port in the United States.

Antoine's famous Baked Alaska hails as its signature dessert, with ice cream encased in pound cake, shrouded in meringue, shaped, smoothed and torched. An elegant touch is the whipped cream signature of "Antoines since 1840," with sketches of little whipped cream birds atop the dessert. Other desserts include *cerises jubilee*, or cherries jubilee, a dream of sweet dark cherries flamed in brandy at the table and served over vanilla ice cream. Cherries jubilee is a flambé dessert considered "fit for a queen," as it was created in the late 1800s to honor England's Queen Victoria during her jubilee celebration.

GELATO/SPUMONI

Angelo Brocato Ice Cream
214 N. Carrollton Avenue
New Orleans

Truly a New Orleans institution since 1905, Angelo Brocato is Louisiana's oldest ice cream shop. Pastel pink walls, wire-backed chairs, tiled archways, marble-topped tables and shelves lined with glass jars filled with delicious treats exude the charm of an old-fashioned Italian parlor.

Angelo Brocato launched his career in an ice cream shop in Palermo beginning at age twelve. After serving in the Italian navy, he was encouraged to immigrate to Louisiana to join his brother Joseph. The Brocato boys worked in sugarcane fields with back-breaking days of hand-cutting cane before opening a family ice cream shop in an Italian neighborhood in New Orleans' French Quarter. Ice cream was prepared during the summer months, while the winter months were dedicated to baking biscotti, cannoli and cookies. Their first ice cream, *torroncino*—a creamy, nougat-based vanilla gelato with toasted almond and cinnamon—was hand-churned and is still served in the shop today. Since ice cream cones were not used in the early days, this luscious gelato was served as a rectangular block and hand-sliced. Though the founder died in 1946, his portrait hangs in the shop, now run by his grandson along with other family members. The shop originally had car hops, mostly Brocato family members, taking orders at a time when families enjoyed their treats by eating in their cars.

Angelo Brocato's keeps the old look of an Italian ice cream parlor with a colorful carousel of gelato to choose from, guaranteeing several returns

Italian cookies served at Louisiana's oldest ice cream shop, Angelo Brocato's in New Orleans. *Courtesy of Angelo Brocato Ice Cream Shop.*

to sample to the tune of twenty-four flavors: pistachio almond, *fiore di latte* (flower of milk), jasmine, *baci* (Italian kiss), amaretto and more.

And the difference between Italian gelato and American ice cream? Although both are delicious, cold treats, gelato has a soft, smooth texture and actually has less fat than ice cream because it contains more milk than cream. It is churned at a slower speed to embrace an intense flavor.

Other Italian cold dishes are sliced rather than scooped for you. Spumoni is a frozen and colorful gelato of pistachio almond, tutti fruiti and lemon with almond whipped cream that is cut into slices. Cassata is similar to spumoni though prepared as a dressed-up cake. And don't forget the pastries: cannoli, twice-baked biscotti and ladyfingers. Many years ago, the crispy, tube-like pastry known as cannoli was filled with ricotta cheese made from sheep or goat milk and was associated with carnival season. A somewhat unusual pastry is the *scadalina*, or *ossa dei morte*, prepared in time for All Saints' Day. These hard "dead man's bone" cookies are flavored with cloves. This unique confection—which actually resembles bones—is a flavored white tube balanced on one side of a flat brown cookie. Many Italian cookies and biscotti are not chewy. Rather they are crunchy in texture and suitable for dipping into wine or coffee.

The shop is a haven for Italian pastries like the *cannocini* (chocolate-dipped custard-filled pastry), flaky *sfogliatelle* and the baba rhum cake, many derived from old family recipes from Sicily.

Brocato's continues to offer a refreshing, semi-frozen drink/dessert known as granita, an Italian fruit ice made from fresh fruit, sugar and water in flavors such as lemon, blood orange, blueberry, strawberry and mango. In the early days, Italian neighbors dropped by Brocato's for breakfast, dipping their warm bread in the freshly made granita to add a little tang.

Root Beer Float

Frostop
Various locations in Louisiana: Laplace, Baton Rouge,
Thibodaux, New Orleans

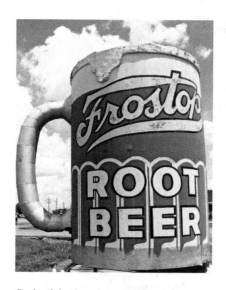

Go back in time for a root beer float at Frostop's. *Photo by author.*

It's a poky place that sends you back in time for drive-in cuisine like burgers and fries, hot dogs and onion rings. The name "Frostop" comes from the signature dessert of the eatery's homemade root beer float of scoops of ice cream drowned by sparkly root beer served in a cold mug. Root beer was created in the mid-1800s by a Philadelphia pharmacist who used a blend of sugar and yeast, roots and barks such as sassafras and sarsaparilla. For miles around, you can spot the iconic fourteen-foot mug, especially at night when the neon lights serve as a beacon to stop by for a nostalgic snack. Frostop started in 1926 in Springfield, Ohio, when L.S. Harvey first concocted the cold treat. Drive-ins were popular for family dining because of the relaxed atmosphere of eating while in your car. The kids often dressed down in their pajamas while they slurped or scooped into the root beer float. This roadside eatery also has an inside dining area for the old rock 'n' rollers to enjoy.

6
Cookies

MACARON COOKIES

This colorful French sandwich cookie has taken the dessert world by storm. Stemming from a royal beginning, the dainty cookie can be traced back to an Italian monastery. An entourage of monks from the monastery traveled to France in 1533 to escort the pastry chefs of Catherine de' Medici upon her marriage to Henry II of France. The chefs showed off their baking skills by introducing the new pastry. The macaron became adored later when two Benedictine nuns known as the Macaron Sisters sought asylum in France during the French Revolution and paid for their room and board by baking and selling these cookies. Who came up with the idea to smash the two cookies together to create a specialty? The simple cookie transitioned into a meringue sandwich cookie in the early twentieth century when Pierre Des Fontaines—the grandson of Louis Ernest Laduree, who founded the Parisian patisserie Laduree—ingeniously sandwiched two macaron cookies with ganache. The name is derived from the word *ammaccare*, meaning "crush," an important step in making the airy cookie, which has crushed almonds as one of its main ingredients.

Sucre
622 Conti
New Orleans

Sucre, named for the French word for sugar, is a Parisian-style sweet shop with several locations in the New Orleans area. The classy boutique bakery with a pastel-themed parlor features an endless assortment of macarons, most notably a New Orleans collection of southern pecan, Bananas Foster, chicory and salted caramel. Lazy summertime and springtime flavors include watermelon, apple pie, blackberry lemon and peaches and cream. Sucre was launched in 2007 by New Orleans restaurateur Joel Dondis, who began his culinary career serving classic French cuisine to his Lake Charles family at age eleven, along with executive pastry chef Tariq Hanna, who proclaims to have "chocolate in his blood."

In creating a bevy of decadent fancies, Sucre also presents a rhapsody of handcrafted chocolates such as the chicory, a New Orleans favorite coffee blend folded into a dark chocolate ganache enrobed in dark chocolate; éclairs; cookies; milkshakes; and gelato. French conversation can be

Hand-crafted macaron cookies at Sucre. *Courtesy of @hannafoto.*

overheard at this patisserie; it's the perfect setting for indulging in fancy coffees and handmade fluffy marshmallows.

Welcome to the good life upstairs at the full-service restaurant called Salon by Sucre, where cocktails are served along with savory sandwiches, cheese and charcuterie and even more delightful desserts. The "pod of gold" is Madagascar chocolate mousse, malted milk chocolate gelato and spiced chocolate croutons encased in a rich chocolate shell.

Pink Cookie

Champagne's Breaux Bridge Bakery
105 South Poydras Street
Breaux Bridge

Connoisseurs of the crumbly cookie differ on what gives this famous pink cookie its distinctive taste. Some guess that the one-hundred-year-old recipe for this delicate sugar cookie with a cream filling hints at a lemony taste. Some say almond; some guess cherry. And some think the secret ingredient is a spoonful or two of French champagne because the vintage bakery in Breaux Bridge, run by the Champagne family (pronounced "shum-pine") since 1888, claims this mystery cookie as its specialty. It has received national attention through Louisiana native son and Cajun musician Hunter Hayes, who proclaimed that Champagne's pink cookies are at the top of what he misses most about home.

It's a jewel of a bakery with quiet times in the kitchen occurring throughout the night, when the magic of mixing and baking takes place. Accompanying the shop's repertoire of baked goods is the unmistakably pleasant aroma of bread baking, which neighbors say reaches them around 5:00 a.m.

Champagne's bakers have come up with other unusual treats. The town of Breaux Bridge is known as "Crawfish Capital of the World." For the town's first crawfish festival over fifty years ago, the bakery created an unforgettable 412-pound cake in the shape of a big crawfish.

There has been some changing of hands in the family-owned bakery since it opened over 125 years ago. The Champagnes first entered the sweets business when George opened the business in 1888. He sold the petite shop to his brother Onezime in 1920. In turn, Onezime sold it to his own son,

Sidney Champagne Sr., in 1933, who in turn passed it to his son Sonny in 1972. Currently, Paul Champagne, fourth generation, has taken over the baking of bread and sweets with daily help from the dough-covered hands of his father, Sonny, prepping at the baking table.

Remodeling through the years has included kitchen upgrades, primarily with the oven and other tools of the trade. The bakery enjoys a nostalgic look and feel of a century-plus-old shop, notably with its brick interior and glass display cases.

Recently, Champagne's opened a second location in the nearby town of Henderson, considered the Gateway to the Atchafalaya Basin, which draws boaters, water skiers and fishermen. Both locations bake a variety of sweets like red coconut balls, banana split cake, pink cake and specialty wedding cakes. Loaves of French bread are stacked on the shelf, right out of the oven.

7

Fruits, Berries and Nuts

PECAN PIE

Nothing says southern hospitality like a neat slice of the classic pecan pie. As one of nature's health foods, the amber-colored pecan stars in this dish, though Louisiana has its own special take on it. We pronounce it "puh-kawn" not "pee-can" for some mysterious (regional) reason. However you may say it, pecans contain more than nineteen vitamins and minerals, and there are over one thousand varieties of pecans. Many cooks use a recipe that includes cane syrup from our own Louisiana sugarcane rather than the standard of corn syrup for the sweet, drippy mix of pecans in a flaky pie crust. Historians attribute the invention of the pecan pie to the newly arrived French settlers in New Orleans in the early 1800s. They were introduced to the nut by Native Americans, who appreciated the wild pecan as a major food source during the autumn. As the only major tree nut that grows naturally in North America, *pecan* comes from a Native American word of Algonquin origin meaning "nut." The first successful grafting of a Centennial pecan was made in 1846 by slave gardener Antoine at Louisiana's Oak Alley Plantation, originally called Bon Sejour, near Darrow, Louisiana.

Roberto's River Road Restaurant
1985 Highway 75
Sunshine

Roberto's is a no-frills café worth the easy drive from Baton Rouge along the historic river road. You'll spot the old place before you get to Carville, home of the National Hansen's Disease Museum. A native of Guatemala City, owner Roberto Sandoval worked at several Baton Rouge restaurants before opening his own in the little community of Sunshine in 2001. Housed in an 1860s building that was once the site of the J.J. LaPlace & Sons General Store, the shabby chic restaurant faces the Mississippi River levee. The store was built during the 1860s by Pierre G. Richard, a seventh-generation descendant of Michel Richard from France. Menu items include grilled fish and other seafood dishes, steaks, soups, dressy salads, burgers, interesting appetizers and crawfish or debris po' boys. As you enter through the rustic door, take in the echo of walking on the old wood floors. Lots of mirrors and old signage from the store add to the casual charm. Lunchtime traffic is usually busy with workers from nearby plants. There's an inviting little bar suitable for letting your hair down. Desserts include Aunt Terri's "happily bursting with nuts" pecan pie as well as flan, lemon cake and king cake bread pudding.

Camellia Grill
540 Chartres Street (French Quarter), New Orleans
626 S. Carrollton Avenue (Uptown), New Orleans

It's an "old school" diner with a big personality—pink walls and shiny doo-dads—especially the marble counter. Your servers are dressed impeccably in whites and a black bowtie as they welcome you to take a seat, entertaining you along the way. You'll get to know your neighbor right off the bat, with seating at swivel bar stools at the U-shaped counters.

There are two locations of this casual eatery in New Orleans. Since 1946, the landmark location on Carrollton has been located on the streetcar line with a look reminiscent of a plantation home supported by four massive columns. The French Quarter location on Chartres has a big window allowing for people-watching—a favorite New Orleans pastime—as pirates,

Camellia Grill, an old-school diner with two locations in New Orleans. *Photo by author.*

saints or others in costume walk by while the city sounds of jazz music blast. Sweaty tourists venture in to the Grill for a cool respite from the Crescent City's humidity.

Both family-friendly spots have giant omelets, "worth waiting for" burgers, gumbo and red beans and rice for breakfast, lunch or dinner. Or drop by for dessert. The Camellia Grill is famous for its "knock your socks off" pecan pie, but there's another variation of this southern dessert. They've lifted up this sweet diva by adding chocolate chips for a masterpiece of a chocolate pecan pie. Even serving it up is a show. A heaping slice is slapped on the griddle upside down with a light pouring of melted butter to boost the taste. The warmed-up wedge is plopped on a plate with a scoop of vanilla ice cream added on, inviting you to scoop up before the whole delight melts away.

STRAWBERRIES

Bless your berry-pickin' heart when you taste the plump scarlet strawberry, recognized as Louisiana's state fruit. Rich in vitamins, low in calories and versatile as a good treat, the strawberry is delicious to eat fresh or cut up in salads, prepared in preserves and used in many desserts. A member of the rose family, the cone-shaped strawberry is available fresh for approximately six months each year and especially prevalent in Tangipahoa and Livingston Parishes.

Ponchatoula Strawberry Festival (April)

One of America's most famous strawberry festivals is hosted by Louisiana's own Ponchatoula since 1971. Ponchatoula, a piney woods village with an

Strawberries take the lead at the Ponchatoula Strawberry Festival. *Photo by author.*

attractive historic downtown, was incorporated six weeks before the outbreak of the Civil War. The local economy depended on farming early on just for local consumption, while also supporting the lumber industry. In the early 1900s, strawberries became commercially viable due to the expansion of the railroad industry—along with refrigerated railcars—leading the way to a cash crop for farmers. With Louisiana boasting more than twenty thousand acres of strawberry farms during the peak year of 1931, it was reported that in one day in April 1931, over 180 rail carloads of strawberries were shipped from this area.

The town has been ambitiously recognized as "Strawberry Capital of the World," where everything strawberry can be found—from aprons to cookie jars, artwork and collectibles. The Ponchatoula Strawberry Festival draws 300,000 visitors annually invited to sample strawberry sangria wine, chocolate-dipped strawberries, fried strawberries or creamy ice cream with strawberry nuggets. It's fun to enjoy the strawberry eating contest, the Strawberry Strut "race" and the Strawberry Ball, a gala with the crowning of a strawberry king and queen. Watch out for the many old trucks filled with pallets of big red strawberries as they ramble down country roads. The entourage is heading out from one of the handful of pick-your-own berry farms, where you can fill buckets of ripe strawberries.

Ponchatoula Strawberry Pie
Courtesy of LouisianaTravel.com

1 quart fresh Ponchatoula strawberries
1 (9-inch) pie shell, baked
1 cup white sugar + ½ tablespoon reserved for whipped cream
3 tablespoons cornstarch
¾ cup water
½ cup heavy whipping cream
¼ teaspoon vanilla extract

Arrange half of strawberries in baked pie shell. Mash remaining berries and combine with sugar in a medium saucepan. Place saucepan over medium heat and bring to a boil, stirring frequently. In a small bowl, whisk together cornstarch and water. Gradually stir cornstarch mixture into boiling strawberry mixture. Reduce heat and simmer until thick, about 10 minutes, stirring occasionally. Pour mixture over berries in the pie shell. Chill for at least two hours. Take whipping cream and beat in a small bowl with ½ tablespoon of sugar and vanilla until peaks form. Spread over top of chilled pie. Cut and serve.

Berrytown Corner Café
100 West Pine Street
Ponchatoula

The brick building that houses this quaint café in downtown Ponchatoula was built in 1904, originally as a pharmacy. Known for miles around for its beignets, the café is open for both breakfast and lunch. The surprise to this fried novelty is discovered at first bite when you taste the delightful strawberry filling inside the beignet. And you can't eat just one of these indulgences. Another dish that the café prepares is strawberry shortcake, which began as a large, sweet biscuit with layers filled with whipped cream and fruit or berries. The shortcake is considered a European concoction of a heavy, though crumbly, pastry. American cooks have been credited with combining the shortcake and luscious strawberries in the mid-1800s, serving the special dish to celebrate the coming of summer.

The café also serves salads topped with strawberries, strawberry malts, refreshing strawberry lemonade and other dishes. In 2012, the eatery entertained the Hollywood scene, as it was the setting for the movie *The Butler*, which starred Oprah Winfrey, Forest Whitaker, Robin Williams and Jane Fonda.

Ambrosia Bakery
8546 Siegen Lane
Baton Rouge

Ambrosia Bakery is a sweets wonderland of an endless display of eye-popping confections like éclairs, king cake, pastries, LSU petit fours—as this is Tiger country—candies, brownies, cookies, breakfast pastries and gelato. Hands-down, one of the showcase desserts is their original fresh strawberry cake, a refreshing four-layer yellow cake with a light filling of whipped cream and chopped fresh strawberries. It's the Sherman family's own version of the strawberry shortcake but more of a cake than a layered pastry that customers go crazy for, especially at Easter and Mother's Day. An added treat are the companion strawberry cut-out cookies, decorated to resemble strawberries. Cheryl Sherman, a certified cake decorator and winner of many international cake competitions, started out by baking cakes from her home. In 1993, with her husband, Felix Sherman, she opened Ambrosia in Louisiana's state capital in a small building that formerly housed a pizza place. With an impressive repertoire of sweets, Ambrosia, which appropriately means "food for the gods," expanded to an 8,200-square-foot facility eight years ago. The bakery palace/deli/coffee shop is also well known for its elaborate wedding cakes and the decadent Zulu King Cake™ filled with chocolate chips, coconut and cream cheese, covered with chocolate icing and topped with toasted coconut.

Blueberries

Mama's Oyster House
608 Front Street
Natchitoches

The charming town of Natchitoches (pronounced Nak-a-tish) was established as a trading post along the Red River in 1714 by French Canadian adventurer Louis Juchereau de St. Denis. Trade was encouraged between the town's namesake, the local Natchitoches Indians, and the Spanish colonists in Mexico. As a result of the Red River course shifting, the town was cut off from its connection to the Mississippi River, forming the thirty-three-mile oxbow lake known as Cane River Lake.

There's a New Orleans feel about the town's historic district, though it is considerably calmer than the Big Easy. Amid the sprinkling of the downtown's wrought-iron accents and French Creole architecture is Front Street, situated along the scenic Cane River. The street retains its brick paving due to the passion of the Association for the Preservation of Historic Natchitoches, a prominent women's group that believed in preserving the historic culture of the area during the 1940s. The determined alliance stopped plans to blacktop the bricked street by literally laying down in front of bulldozers, causing the work to stop. This occurred during the administration of Governor Earl Long, who eventually supported the women's actions and sent state workers home to halt any removal of the historic bricks.

Located on Front Street in a long and narrow building dating to the late 1800s is Mama's Oyster House, a perfect setting for a picturesque view of the Cane River, especially during the Annual Christmas Festival of Lights. Since 1927, this six-week festival transforms the historic district along the river into an unforgettable winter wonderland with 300,000 lights decorating water structures on the river. Other entertainment includes a parade, a tour of homes, fireworks and musical performances.

Mama's Oyster House was opened in 2000 and features a rustic tavern setting connected with a blues room for live music. Mama's is lit up with neon beer advertising signs and decorated in hunters' décor. Lively conversation can be heard among customers who range from bikers, families and weekenders who come in for po' boys, oysters on the half-shell, pasta and cold beer. For dessert, there's a summertime blueberry crunch. The sapphire-colored blueberry is a good source of fiber and vitamin C and ready for picking in Louisiana from May through mid-June. Mama's cool crunch dessert has three layers: a crumbly streusel-like crust filled with sweet and bright blueberry compote and topped with whipped cream.

MAYHAW

A bit of a mystery berry, the wonderful mayhaw is used to prepare Louisiana's state jelly, mayhaw berry.

It is sometimes mistakenly called "mayhog," which it's not. Native to Louisiana, the berry thrives in the wild in boggy areas. The mayhaw, roughly the size of a cherry, resembles a crabapple with a color variation from pink to dark red to yellow. The "liquid gold" jelly is truly worth its weight in gold, so desirable is it for making desserts, wine, syrup or jelly for slathering on hot biscuits or toast. The taste can be compared to an overripe apple, sweet but a little tart.

Harvested in May, the berry grows on a hawthorne tree. Because of the numerous thorns on the trees, harvesting can be challenging. One way to gather the berries is by placing a bed sheet under the trees and shaking the trunk like all get-out until the nuggets fall. The mayhaw is about as southern as you can get, with trees growing in the wild from East Texas to Georgia. It has gained popularity for its health benefits, as it provides a good source of antioxidants in preventing disease. The trees can reproduce from seeds that are left on the ground and scattered by birds and squirrels.

Mayhaws were once known as thorny hawthornes and grew only in swamps, though now they enjoy a popular role in home gardens and family orchards. They may serve as an ornamental tree in landscape plans, especially the "Maxine" variety. The trees are long-lived and may produce berries for more than fifty years.

Members of the Louisiana Mayhaw Association, responsible for promoting the southern tradition of the native mayhaw, recognize the unusual beauty and taste of the berry. Two Louisiana towns honor the flavorful berry by hosting an annual mayhaw festival. The town of Marion in Union Parish has hosted one since 1982, and it's worth the trip to North Louisiana for the turkey calling contest, mayhaw spitting contest and mayhaw jelly cooking contest. The town of Starks in Calcasieu Parish puts on a celebration of the mayhaw that includes gospel singing performances. Many home cooks proudly sell jars filled using their own recipes for homemade mayhaw jelly.

Blueberry Hill Farm
5121 Bellevue Road
Haughton

No scarecrow oversees this farm, just eighty-seven-year-old Mac "Wendell" McCoskey and his dog Petey tagging along to watch over the ten-acre farm where families love to picnic. He hosts family outings, welcoming kids to pick blueberries, blackberries and other fruit, sneaking in a sample along the way. Blueberry Hill Farm is populated with mayhaw trees, too (all the berries cover seven acres), and a vegetable garden with big cucumbers and butterbeans. A farm boy from Iowa, Mac moved to Louisiana for milder winters after retiring from the U.S. Air Force. He likes to use the mayhaw pulp to make marinades and reports that the distinctive jelly is good on pancakes. When purchasing his first mayhaw tree from the local county agent many years ago, he was surprised how small the sapling was. He planted the trees twenty feet apart in a wet area at the bottom of the property and learned that you couldn't kill it, so hardy is it even through winter. From the swamp to the orchard and into the jelly jar—Mac does have mayhaw jelly available at this homey roadside stand, one mile east of Louisiana Downs Racetrack.

Mayhaw Cream Cheese Pie
Courtesy of Diana Vincent Callahan

Pie

1 cup mayhaw pulp
½ cup sugar
1 tablespoon cornstarch
1 tablespoon cold water
1 (8-ounce) package cream cheese
1 (9-inch) graham cracker pie crust

Topping

Mayhaw jelly
Whipped topping

Mix pulp and sugar. Mix the cornstarch and cold water separately, then add to the heated pulp mixture. Add cream cheese and beat until smooth. Cook until it thickens and pour into crust. Chill until cold before serving. For topping, mix 2 to 4 tablespoons of mayhaw jelly with prepared whipped topping.

BANANAS FOSTER

Brennan's
417 Royal Street
New Orleans

It's another example of New Orleans turning a surplus into something special—in this case, the tropical banana. New Orleans became the top U.S. banana port in the early 1900s, with bunches coming in from Central and South America.

During the early 1950s, Owen Brennan—Brennan's Restaurant owner at the time—challenged his chef Paul Blangé to create a new dessert using bananas because his younger brother John had an oversupply of bananas in his produce company. A flambéed dessert was created that continues to be a showstopper at each command performance at Brennan's. An honor was bestowed on Brennan's friend and frequent customer Richard Foster by naming the famous dish after him. Ralph Brennan (John's son) is current owner of the deluxe eatery and is a third-generation restaurateur.

Bananas Foster is a delicious boozy dessert of sliced bananas, butter, cinnamon, banana liqueur, rum and brown sugar that is quick to prepare. The tableside preparation of the indulgence acts as a dramatic finale to a grand meal at this fine dining restaurant known for its French and Creole dishes. Over thirty-five thousand pounds of bananas are flamed and sautéed in South American rum at Brennan's each year. Bananas are peeled and simmered in bubbling syrup, and in a flash, tall flames appear for a few minutes. Then poof! Everything settles down in anticipation of the scooping of warm bananas onto a mound of ice cream.

The flaming Bananas Foster dessert, the finale to a grand meal. *Courtesy of Brennan's Restaurant.*

Bananas Foster
Courtesy of Brennan's

1 ounce butter
½ cup light brown sugar
¼ teaspoon cinnamon
1 ½ ounces banana liqueur
½ banana per guest
1 ½ ounces aged rum
Ice cream

Combine butter, sugar and cinnamon in a flambé pan. As the butter melts under medium heat, add the banana liqueur and stir to combine. As the sauce starts to cook, peel and add the bananas to the pan. Cook the bananas until they begin to soften, about one to two minutes. Tilt back the pan to slightly heat the far edge. Once hot, carefully add the rum and tilt the pan toward the flame to ignite the rum. Stir the sauce to ensure that all of the alcohol cooks out. Serve cooked bananas over ice cream and top with the sauce in the pan. Serves 2 to 4.

8
Other

CRÈME BRÛLÉE

So sophisticated is this baked concoction of egg yolks, cream and sugar that it is best served in individual dishes. A light layer of sugar is sprinkled on top then caramelized under a broiler or kitchen torch. The topping has a light crunch when your spoon makes its way to the smooth custard beneath.

As early as the Middle Ages, ingenious cooks from France, England and Spain have staked claims to creating this dish. Spain's version was called *crema catalane*, while burnt cream desserts were prepared at England's Trinity College in Cambridge in 1879.

Houmas House Plantation and Gardens
40136 Highway 942
Darrow

The Houmas House has a noteworthy history that began when the first owners of the plantation, the Houmas Indians, received a land grant to occupy the fertile plain between the Mississippi River and Lake Maurepas. In turn, it was sold to Maurice Conway and Alexander Latil in the mid-1700s. Construction of the massive Greek Revival mansion with its fourteen classic Doric columns was completed in 1828. An earlier French provincial house built by Latil is situated directly behind the mansion, adjoined by a carriageway. Considered the grande dame on the historic Great River Road along the Mississippi River, the Houmas Plantation was once America's largest sugar producer, with ninety-eight thousand dedicated acres. As a survivor through wars, flooding and a desperate state of disrepair for several years, the Houmas House was restored to its former glory when New Orleans businessman and historian Kevin Kelly acquired it in 2003. Tours of the lush grounds and magnificent estate are available for visitors to view a glimpse of the past. Dining choices in the restaurant range from casual to Sunday brunch and fine dining. Overnight lodging is available in twenty-one cottages, gloriously furnished in a period style when the Houmas House was known as the Sugar Palace.

Chefs at the restaurants at Houmas House take a spirited spin on the French dessert custard with their decadent Chocolate Wild Turkey Crème Brûlée. Another top-notch dessert is the Mint Julep Crème Brûlée, which ties in with the South's classic sweet cocktail.

Chocolate Wild Turkey Crème Brûlée
Courtesy of the Houmas House Plantation

3 ounces dark chocolate, finely chopped
¼ cup tablespoons sugar
1 ¼ cups heavy cream
1 vanilla bean, split
1 ½ cups Wild Turkey bourbon whiskey
10 egg yolks

Preheat oven to 300 degrees. Place the chopped chocolate in a small bowl. Set aside.

In a saucepan over medium heat, bring sugar, heavy cream, split vanilla bean and Wild Turkey to a simmer. Once the mixture starts to get foamy, remove from heat. Take out the vanilla bean halves and scrape out the seeds, adding the seeds back to the mixture. Pour the mixture over the chopped chocolate and let sit for a minute. Gently stir until the chocolate is completely melted. Slowly pour half of the chocolate mixture into the eggs while whisking.

Continue to whisk, and slowly pour in the remaining chocolate mixture. Add another drop if needed. Strain the custard into a spouted measuring cup. Evenly divide the custard between 4 ramekins. Place the ramekins into a baking dish. Pour boiling water into the baking dish until the water comes up to about the custard level. Bake 25 to 60 minutes, depending on the size of the ramekin, or until the custard is set (it should still be jiggly in the center). Remove the baking dish from the oven and let the ramekins cool in the water bath. Transfer to the refrigerator and chill for at least 4 hours. Once chilled, sprinkle a generous amount of sugar on the top of each custard. Using a kitchen torch, caramelize the sugar. Let sit for 5 minutes before serving.

Makes 4 servings.

TIRAMISU

Tiramisu is a lyrical name for a classic Italian dessert that literally means "pick-me-up." Likely this refers to the two caffeinated ingredients that are used in preparing this layered treat: coffee and chocolate. Credit goes to the Italians, who first prepared this lovely sweet in the 1960s.

Preparation begins with a layering of ladyfingers, light, sponge-like biscuits that are slightly sweet. A thorough soaking with liqueur adds the special touch. A custardy topping of mascarpone cheese, espresso, eggs and sugar is added with a scattering of cocoa powder on top. Ladyfingers, or *savoiardi*, were developed at the court of the Duchy of Savoy during the fifteenth century to welcome the king of France.

Mona Lisa
1212 Royal Street
New Orleans

Tiramisu is the celebrated dessert prepared in-house at this neighborhood café tucked away in a quiet area of Royal Street, away from the antique shops. Versions of the smiling da Vinci masterpiece grace the walls in a variety of amusing depictions. Long and narrow, comforting in its Italian simplicity, the intimate eatery was once part of a carriage repair shop.

Bountiful pasta dishes, pizza, wine and other Italian staples have graced the menu since 1983. Slow down the pace with a short walk from Bourbon Street to find red-checked tablecloths, subtle golden-hued walls and fancy chandeliers to set the stage for an enchanting feast. Ciao!

GERMAN SWEETS

Crystal Weddings
110 Mimosa Place
Lafayette

Roberts Cove German Heritage Museum and Germanfest
7121 Roberts Cove Road
Rayne

As they say in Germany, *Willkomen*. Likewise it's a common greeting in Roberts Cove, a German community in southwest Louisiana. In 1867, Reverend Peter Leonhard Thevis, a native priest of the Geilenkirchen area of Germany, was assigned to a New Orleans church parish to serve the growing population of German immigrants. Years later, some of his family traveled to America, eventually making their way to the town of Rayne. A nearby stretch of prairie land was named Roberts Cove in honor of surveyor Benjamin Roberts, who had mapped out the settlement.

In 1880, the original settlers of Roberts Cove were joined by other Germans who had fled their homeland of Gangelt, Geilenkirchen, near the Dutch border with Germany. These large families desired a better way of life for themselves and their children in their search for religious tolerance, avoidance of military conflicts and a quest to retain their livelihood as farmers. By relocating to Louisiana, they developed fields for rice farming and spreads for raising cattle while embracing their old-world customs, German language and Catholic culture.

To preserve their heritage and support a historical museum, the people of Roberts Cove host a Germanfest that began in 1995. Thousands of visitors attend the festival, taking a leap into the past through a museum with wonderful resources of family history and photos pertaining to

Roberts Cove Germanfest features beer, music, dancing and German cuisine. *Photo by author.*

descendants of the thirty-six original families along with rotating displays of beer steins, branding irons and maps of Germany pinpointing the origin of these families.

Zucher Platschen (Sugar Cookie)

October's Germanfest in Roberts Cove celebrates the richness of the German culture—complete with singers and dancing of the polka, accordion music, lots of beer and traditional sweets like the *zucher platschen* (sugar cookie). Crumbly, buttery and the right size for a child-size indulgence, the sugar cookie derived from an earlier, unleavened cookie called a "jumble" in Europe, which gained popularity during the seventeenth and eighteenth centuries. This unleavened food could be dried and stored for many months and transported easily. During the 1930s, children began setting out these fancies along with a glass of milk to welcome Santa Claus on Christmas Eve. In Roberts Cove, a celebration commemorating St. Nicholas Day on December 5 continues with visits made to children to give out sweets.

Mary Boudreaux, owner of Crystal Weddings Bakery in Lafayette, is descended from the Cramer family, one of the original settlers of Roberts Cove. Last year, she spread joy throughout Germanfest through the twenty-four thousand cookies she baked. It's a popular dessert from the Mother Country because the ingredients are readily available with a simple taste, though quite appealing. The dough is easy to work with and can be dressed up with frosting or sprinkles.

Zucker Platschen
Courtesy of Roberts Cove Germanfest Cookbook

I cup butter
2¼ cups sugar
¼ cup milk
2 eggs
I teaspoon vanilla
4 cups flour
3 teaspoons baking powder

Cream butter and sugar. Blend milk, eggs and vanilla. Mix with butter mixture. Sift flour and baking powder together. Gradually add to creamed mixture. Separate into 4 sections. Roll very thin on sugar/floured surface (use I½ cups each). Cut into circles with the mouth of a glass. Bake at 350 degrees for 10 minutes or until lightly brown. Cool completely. Store in airtight containers.

Apple Kuchen

Apple kuchen, or *apfelkuchen*, is another Germanfest dessert. *Kuchen* means "cake" in German, although in America we consider it a one-layered round coffee cake that may be served for breakfast or dessert. It's usually a yeast-risen and moderately sweet cake or bun with nuts, raisins and aromatic spices such as cinnamon, nutmeg and cloves. Variations may include fillings and glazes, along with a streusel crumb topping or sprinkling of powdered sugar. The reward of the apple kuchen are the chunks of the tart apple as filling, which add juices to the dough so it remains moist.

Fruitcake

Another German treat from this community associated with the merry time of the Christmas season is the fruitcake, or *fruchtebrot*. American comedian Johnny Carson often joked that there was actually only one fruitcake ever made in history and it had been passed around year after year for centuries. Actually, the fruitcake is well loved as a traditional German dessert and not considered a holiday reject. Josie Berken Thevis, curator of the Roberts Cove German Heritage Museum and a descendant of one of the original settlers of the community, noted that the tradition of baking a fruitcake was something she learned from her mother and now shares with her sisters and nieces. Usually the family bakes a few small loaves as gifts and one larger one to serve at Christmas along with coffee. It seems the cake improves by letting it sit for a week before cutting into the chunks of pineapple, green and red cherries, chopped dates and chopped pecans that are the mainstay of her family cake. The process takes cracking a lot of eggs along with stiff egg beating. A glaze of apple juice and spiced rum is brushed over the cake to keep it moist.

As preparation of the fruitcake can be time-consuming, it was considered a dessert of indulgence during medieval times. Many ingredients may be used, including currants or raisins, a variety of nuts, citrus peel, bits of candied fruit, dates, cherries and liqueur such as brandy. A mix of spices such as cinnamon or cloves was often used to prepare this cake, which improves with age. Some variations used honey as a way to tint the cake to a dark coloring. The cake was commonly baked in a round tin ring.

Light Fruitcake
Courtesy of Josie Thevis

2 cups pecans, coarsely cut
1 pound candied cherries, ½ green, ½ red, chopped
1 pound candied pineapple
1 box chopped dates
1 cup golden raisins
1¾ cups flour
1 cup butter, room temperature
1 cup sugar
5 large eggs

1 ¼ teaspoons baking powder
½ teaspoon salt
1 tablespoon vanilla extract
1 tablespoon lemon extract or juice of 1 lemon

Mix chopped nuts, chopped cherries, pineapple pieces, dates and raisins in medium mixing bowl. Dredge with ½ cup of the flour. Set aside. Cream butter and sugar until light and fluffy, add eggs one at a time. Sift together remaining flour, baking powder and salt. Fold into egg and butter mixture. Add vanilla and lemon. Mix. Add fruit and nut to mixture. Pour into greased and floured pans. Bake at 350 degrees in 8- by 4-inch or 9- by 5-inch loaf pans for 65 to 75 minutes or 300 degrees for small pans 45 minutes or until done.

HUNGARIAN SWEETS

Hungarian Settlement Historical Society
Albany, LA

Louisiana is truly a melting pot drawing in flavors and cultures of all kinds. That's why the Bayou State is so renowned for its culinary delights. Although likely more known for its French settlers, there were many other nationalities that were part of a mass migration of people to Louisiana.

During the mid- to late 1800s, the occurrence of wars, strife and food shortages made living in Hungary nearly impossible. The Hungarians, also known as Magyars, began looking for a better life. Many arrived by ship to enter Ellis Island, choosing to pack up their belongings and leave their jobs and homes in the quest to improve their social conditions. Most Hungarian immigrants settled in the northern cities of New York City, Cleveland and Chicago. Others moved farther south and settled in the states of Pennsylvania, West Virginia, New Jersey and Virginia.

In 1896, a group of three adventurous Hungarians ventured south to find work in the sawmill industry after learning that Brackenridge Lumber had purchased thousands of acres of pine forest in southeastern Louisiana to clear-cut the timber. To entice more Hungarians to come south, Adam Mocsary, Tivador Zboray and Gyula Bruskay worked hand-in-hand with the lumber company to promote the opportunity to purchase twenty-acre tracts of land. The three gentlemen founded the community of Hungarian Settlement (Árpádhon), now called Albany, in Livingston Parish. Believing in the promise of a mild climate, honest work at the mill and a chance to own land, many other Hungarians moved to Louisiana. By 1935, there were three hundred Hungarian families in the area. In time, raising strawberries as a cash crop was developed for this area.

The community of Hungarian Settlement is considered the largest rural Hungarian settlement in the United States today. To preserve the Hungarian culture, two organizations were formed. In 1976, the Árpádhon Hungarian Settlement Cultural Association was established to showcase Hungarian food and culture by maintaining an annual harvest dance, which began in 1912. The tightknit families share their culture in many ways—by bringing in their native dances accompanied by authentic folk music and introducing their country's breads, pastries and other delicacies. Dancers are dressed in white costumes adorned in red, white and green, which are the colors of Hungary's flag. The mission of transforming an old school building into a museum was undertaken by the Hungarian Settlement Historical Society in 2000. Still a work in progress, the museum will display costumes,

Hungarian kalács, a nut-filled pastry. *Courtesy of Alex and Royanne Kropog.*

memorabilia, maps and historic photos of farms, sawmills and families to portray the fascinating lifestyle of the Hungarian culture of the Albany area.

Many in Hungarian Settlement carry on cooking traditions taught by their parents and grandparents. Among the baked treasures they have contributed to Louisiana are sweet dishes such as *kalács*, a nut-filled pastry especially popular during Christian holidays. The yeast dough is rolled thin and filled with nuts, sweetened poppy seed and even jams. Once baked, the rolls are cut into slices for serving. They are also known as *beigli*.

Palacsinta, a delightful dish, is another popular Hungarian dessert. It's a glamorous, thin version of a pancake that may be filled with cottage cheese, fruit or fruit jam. It may be rolled or folded into triangles.

Kalács
Courtesy of Alex and Royanne Kropog

Dough

2 packages yeast
⅓ cup warm water
½+ cup sugar
6 cups flour
½ teaspoon salt
1 stick butter
4 egg yolks
1 cup warm milk
1 teaspoon vanilla

Nut Filling

1+ pound pecans or walnuts
Sugar to taste
5 beaten egg whites
1 handful raisins, soaked in warm water and drained
1 teaspoon vanilla or lemon extract

Put yeast and ⅓ cup warm water with a little sugar into a covered bowl and let sit for 5 minutes. Put flour, salt, butter, egg yolks, sugar and yeast into mixer bowl and attach dough hook. Start mixer on no. 1 and add warm milk and vanilla slowly until well blended and dough begins to collect on the dough hook and no flour is left in bottom of bowl. Add a little milk if needed. Knead the dough on no. 2 speed for at least 5 minutes or until dough becomes elastic and the right consistency.

Remove dough from mixer and place into bowl, covering with a clean cloth. Place in a warm place and let rise for an hour. After dough has risen, divide into 5 parts. Roll dough thin, about the length of the pan it will bake in and about 10 inches wide. Continually work the dough as you roll it into a rectangular shape.

For nut filling, grind nuts with food grinder or food chopper. Add sugar, egg whites, raisins and extract to form a thick paste.

Spread nut mixture evenly on top. Roll and tuck ends under, placing in a greased pan. Cover with a clean cloth and let rise for 15 minutes before baking. Brush tops with milk wash before baking in a 350-degree oven for 25 to 30 minutes until golden brown. Cover with a cloth for 20 minutes to let cool. The rolls can be cut into slices for serving. Kalács freeze well.

Palacsinta
Hungarian Crepe Suzettes
Courtesy of Alex and Royanne Kropog

3 eggs
¼ cup sugar
Dash of salt
½ teaspoon vanilla
1 ⅛ cup flour
Milk (enough to make pourable)

Beat eggs. Add sugar, salt and vanilla. Beat well. Add flour, beat until smooth and add milk until thin. Fry in Teflon skillet using only a little oil. Fill with cottage cheese (sweetened to taste) or fresh fruit jam. Roll and place in a covered casserole dish. Place in warm oven at 300 degrees for a few minutes to heat thoroughly but not enough to cook. Serve with Cool Whip, strawberries or fruit of choice—good as a breakfast dish or dessert.

ST. JOSEPH'S DAY ALTAR

A cornucopia of cultures within Louisiana has influenced the intermingling of traditions and cuisine, making us all the richer. An influx of Italians, especially Sicilians, immigrated to Louisiana, arriving at the Port of New Orleans in the 1800s. Many found work on sugar plantations, taking over duties from the newly freed slaves. Some became farmers, while others opened fruit and vegetable roadside stands that later became corner stores.

One of the fascinating traditions from the Old Country is the celebration of St. Joseph's Day Altar on March 19 with the display of an elaborate altar in many Catholic churches in Louisiana. Many centuries ago, the families of Sicily experienced a long period of drought and famine. In desperation, they prayed to St. Joseph, the patron saint of Sicily, for his help and intercession. Miraculously, the rains came, and crops were nourished in answer to their prayers. In thanksgiving, offerings were made to St. Joseph by erecting and decorating a lovely altar. In addition, a promise was made to share the riches of the St. Joseph Day's Altar by feeding the poor and hungry.

Small bags of fava beans were handed out as keepsakes to visitors during the event. These lucky beans, once raised in Sicily, were considered cattle fodder, but they also served as a nourishing snack for farmers. Legend says that you will never be broke as long as you have the lucky fava bean.

Although the Louisiana practice of St. Joseph's Day Altars was primarily centered in New Orleans, the custom was introduced to the southern part of the state during World War II. Father Michael Russo, a Louisiana native of Sicilian descent, began hosting the Italian St. Joseph's Day Altar twenty-seven years ago when he served as associate pastor of St. Joseph Roman Catholic Church in Rayne. Displaying this special altar comes from a promise he made that as long as he was a priest, he would always host this practice, which is continued at his current parish, Our Lady of Fatima Catholic Church in Lafayette. He recalls that in Morgan City, Louisiana, where he grew up, St. Joseph's Day Altars were held primarily in homes as an offering to ask for help with family illnesses or personal hardships.

Father Russo attributes Louisiana's love of the Sicilian custom of the altar to the way it revolves around food and generosity to those less fortunate. As the tradition of the altar spreads to more Louisiana churches, parishioners look forward to planning and baking goods to place at the altar. Meatless spaghetti with an addition of boiled eggs and treats similar to what is displayed on the altar are shared with the community. No meat dishes are included on the altar because when the St. Joseph's Day Altar tradition began following

The cannoli, a special filling in a rolled-up pastry shell. *Courtesy of Angelo Brocato Ice Cream Shop.*

the drought, cattle were scarce. Rather than sprinkling cheese over pasta dishes, toasted Italian breadcrumbs (*mudica*) were used to represent sawdust as a reminder that St. Joseph was a carpenter.

As a work of art with simple draping in white, the St. Joseph's Day Altar is constructed in three tiers to represent the Holy Trinity. Many hours are spent in dressing the bountiful altar with flowers, fruit, vegetables, seafood, votive candles and statues of the Holy Family. Elaborate loaves of breads and cakes are designed and may be shaped as a lamb or rosary cake while a loaf of bread is formed as a carpenter's tool to represent the profession of St. Joseph. Delicacies include cannoli, biscotti iced in colors of pink, green or white and a variety of cookies such as cocoons, which are sugared shortbreads. Other specialties include Italian fig cookies, sesame seed cookies and fried cookies known as *pignolata*, which resemble pinecones to serve as a reminder of the pinecones that Jesus played with as a child.

Cocoons
Courtesy of Mary Rogers Thibeaux, Lafayette, Louisiana

½ cup real butter, room temperature
¼ cup confectioners sugar
¼ teaspoon vanilla
1 ¼ cups flour
¾ cup finely chopped pecans

Cream butter and sugar and vanilla together. Mix in flour and pecans. Shape into cocoons, crescents or balls. Bake in a 325-degree oven for 20 minutes. While still warm, sprinkle or roll in more powdered sugar. Makes 3 ½ dozen.

9

Pies and Cobblers

ICEBOX PIES

Ah, the days of simple life before our dependence on kerosene lamps for lighting and an icebox to temporarily store perishables. The original icebox was a metal or wooden cupboard. Blocks of ice weighing between twenty-five and fifty pounds were wrapped in thick material like burlap and delivered by wagon from icehouse to households. A big challenge was the small size of the icebox along with keeping ice cold enough, especially during the summer months. The majority of Louisiana folks were farmers, and many did not have electricity until after World War II.

Hardworking families enjoyed the pleasure of dessert after a hearty evening meal. Rather than heating up the house by turning on the oven to prepare a grand finale for their supper, homemakers looked for lighter, cool desserts, especially for those sticky times of summer. The versatility of the icebox pie guaranteed its popularity, as a variety of fruit fillings could be experimented with to perk it up. The simple blend of eggs, sweetened condensed milk and fruit—whether blueberry, lemon or strawberry—could all be poured into a graham cracker crust and topped with whipped cream. These pies were simple to make yet suitable for chilling in the icebox or in the freezer once families progressed to commercial refrigerators with freezers at the top.

Strawn's Eat Shop
125 E. Kings Highway
Shreveport

Strawn's Eat Shop delights with the cool creaminess of its lofty pies—butterscotch, chocolate, banana cream and seasonal flavors of pumpkin and peach. And this is one you won't forget: divine strawberry icebox pie, with layers of fresh strawberry wedges that are topped with frothy, homemade whipped cream. Strawn's make the choice easy for you; buy a slice or the whole pie.

Eye-catching murals of celebrities grace the wall, but the real art is the pie. Aside from icebox pies, Strawn's is known for grandma cooking like fried chicken, meatloaf, beef stew and cornbread. Every Friday during the school year, there is a spectacle to behold when students from nearby Byrd High School parade in for breakfast beginning at 5:30 a.m. The regular customers come and go in shifts, casually nodding to the veteran waiters to confirm that they want their usual order. Other special events occur throughout the year on a whim. On Independence Day, a skit is performed, complete with Thomas Jefferson reading the Declaration of Independence, all with the backdrop of a family setting.

The laid-back eatery with its nostalgic look has been located in a charming historic district of Shreveport since it opened in 1944 across from Centenary College. The Gauthier family bought out the diner in 1988, expanding from 50 to 150 seats. The Food Network featured this Shreveport treasure as a top place to visit for good eats. It sports a friendly atmosphere where you can gaze at the cooks performing their magic at the griddle cooking bacon and fried eggs for breakfast. Dishes of butter are set on the counter, handy for helping yourself to dab on fluffy pancakes or southern biscuits.

Key Lime Pie

Key lime pie is a tart lime-flavored custard topped with meringue or whipped cream. The look is similar to lemon meringue, though tinted light green in color. Native to Southeast Asia, the key lime, a fruit, was introduced to America by explorer Christopher Columbus. The key lime pie was immortalized in the Florida Keys, as this was an area where few cows grazed and fresh milk was not readily available. Then there was the timely introduction of sweetened condensed milk to American homemakers by Gail Borden in 1856. These circumstances contributed to the creation of the tropical key lime pie. Legend says that Aunt Sally, a cook for ship salvager and Florida's first homegrown millionaire, William Curry, used canned milk in several recipes and concocted the delicious pie. The creamy mix of key lime juice, eggs and condensed milk is complemented by either a crust of graham crackers or a pastry crust. Throughout the South—and as the state pie of Florida—key lime pie remains a cool dessert that does not require baking.

Blue Southern Comfort Foods
5863 Fairfield Avenue
Shreveport

One of the specialties of Blue Southern Comfort Foods is the revved-up key lime pie that owner Carolyn Manning Simmons whips up. The tropical pie, really the whole café, started as a dream come true for Carolyn. She has ventured into many careers, from dabbling in real estate to building and running an indoor soccer facility. Finally, she came around to dedicating her career to what she wanted to do all along, which was to become a chef, though not your run-of-the-mill chef. As pit master extraordinaire, using wood and hickory for grilling or smoking, she specializes in dishes such as pulled pork served over grits, buffalo wings and a wild made-to-order hamburger.

Growing up, Carolyn dined mostly on canned goods and frozen pizza, as admittedly, her mother may not have been an adventurous cook. As part of a military family, Carolyn was introduced to the world of global dishes, which piqued her interest in experiencing a bounty of cuisines. When she came across her family's treasured cookbook from the 1950s, *The Joy of Cooking*, it presented possibilities of wild experiments in the kitchen.

Many of her early baking trials stemmed from her grandmother's recipes, including apple strudel, the basis for Carolyn's own rendition of king cake. Carolyn's do over in life included selling her baked goods at a local farmers' market. This led to opening a startup catering company, which exposed her to the movie business when she cooked for movie crews coming into Shreveport.

An opportunity came to light when a Shreveport building that had once housed a hospital flower shop was available for sale. With less than $100 in her bank account, Carolyn took a leap of faith in 2013 when she purchased the building and opened up her own fabulous café. A bright star on the local food scene and now in another location, Blue Southern Comfort Foods serves a variety of dishes, such as smoked meats and pizza (customers are partial to pulled pork pizza). Her key lime pie is her signature sweet, although she has a carrot cake cheesecake that is also flashy.

Her culinary creativity came through when after experimenting with recipes and techniques, her grilled mushroom burger placed her talents in the national spotlight with the James Beard Foundation's Better Burger Project competition.

CANE RIVER CREAM PIE

Lasyone's Meat Pie Restaurant
622 Second Street
Natchitoches

It's a down-home diner famous for its savory meat pie that also boasts a one-of-a-kind mile-high confection called the Cane River Cream Pie. As the house special, the pie is a wobbly chocolate mess with a flaky crust and a whipped topping worthy of satisfying anyone's sweet tooth. This darling of a dish with a hint of chocolate spice was created in honor of the thirty-mile-long Cane River, which runs through the charming historic town of Natchitoches. Located in northwest Louisiana, the town—established in 1714—is the oldest permanent settlement in the Louisiana Purchase.

James Lasyone, the son of a sharecropper, remembered tales of the north Louisiana tradition of vendors selling toasty meat pies at roadside stands since the early 1900s. While spending twenty-five years as a butcher in a grocery shop, he always dreamed of starting his own business. Taking the memory of these delicious pies and with a scant $6.95 pocketful of change, he opened his own sit-down restaurant in 1967. Lasyone's features the deep-fried pork and beef meat pies as well as southern favorites like fried chicken, red beans and rice and loads of vegetable sides.

Now run by Lasyone's daughter, this landmark eatery located in the historic district is adjacent to the 1896 courthouse and across from the 1857 Immaculate Conception Church. When the movie *Steel Magnolias* was filmed in this lovely town in 1989, Lasyone's drew rave reviews from movie cast members Sally Field, Dolly Parton, Julia Roberts and Shirley MacLaine.

PEACH COBBLER

Summertime's fleshy fruit, the peach, is native to China and was originally called "Persian apple" by the Romans. Columbus is given credit for bringing the peach to America during his second and third voyages to the New World. A popular way to prepare the peach in a dessert is the cobbler or variations known by such colorful names of buckle, crisp or betty.

Peach cobbler was a novel sweet dish of early American pioneers. Ever resourceful, they looked for fruits and berries that were easily available. The colonial homemakers poured fruit like peaches into a covered black iron pot. To rustle up a messy crust, spoonfuls of dough were dropped on top of the fruit, making the dish look cobbled rather than smooth. As the cobbler baked over an open fire, the filling stewed within its own juices, allowing the pastry to puff up. The beauty of the cobbler is that with the right proportions of crust and fruit, a scrappy topping doesn't matter. It's okay to serve it in a muddled state. Just kick up the hot baked treat a bit by adding a scoop of ice cream and allow the fruit to shine through.

Morel's Restaurant
210 Morrison Parkway
New Roads

Seated at Morel's, you'd be hard-pressed to garner a better view to watch the Fourth of July fireworks along False River, the twenty-two-mile oxbow lake that serves as a paradise for water sports. Morel's Restaurant, with its floor-to-ceiling windows, is at a prime location for waterside dining—next to the public boat landing.

The town of New Roads was established in 1822 when Catherine Depau, a free woman of color, opened and developed a six-block subdivision at the

Restaurant in Morel Hotel in New Roads, opened in 1926. *Courtesy of Brian J. Costello.*

front of her False River plantation. As the parish seat in Pointe Coupee Parish, New Roads is one of the oldest settlements in the Mississippi Valley and is enjoyed as a haven for those seeking the best of bass, bream and catfish. Others enjoy swimming and sporting around on jet skis. A bit of a sleepy town (meaning relaxing), New Roads upholds a pleasant downtown with neighborhoods of Creole and Victorian homes.

This "off the beaten path" town has enjoyed special events such as Mardi Gras since 1897, boat parades, fishing rodeos and firework shows during New Year's Eve from the many camps along the river in New Roads, as well as from the adjacent community of Ventress.

The Morel family has been in Louisiana since 1847, having played an important role in the hospitality industry since 1926 through a restaurant they operated. Fast-forward to 1982, when schoolteacher Georgia Morel and her husband, Buddy, a rancher, accepted an opportunity to take over a small bait shop located on the river and they reeled it in, hook, line and sinker.

And the little bait shop unexpectedly transformed into something more when fishermen came in to buy bait and tackle and requested "a sandwich to pack for lunch while out on the water." Then, "how about something hot like gumbo?" In consideration of customer requests, the Morels outgrew the bait shop and built a sizable restaurant adjacent to the public boat launching and pier. Now you get an entourage of diners propelling in for lunch by boat for seafood, po' boys, salads and the convenience of a grab and go lunch. To accommodate visitors, the Morels also have an adjacent twelve-room inn and an antique shop where Georgia specializes in American primitives and Buddy displays his restored early electric light fixtures.

A spectacular sunset view and a grand meal lead to a memorable dessert. Hat's off to Morel's desserts of crème brûlée topped with fruit, hot and toasty peach cobbler à la mode, bread pudding and other specialties.

Louisiana Peach Festival (June)
Ruston

Smack dab in the middle of the rolling hills of rich farmland in North Louisiana is the town of Ruston, a good setting for growing whopping big peaches for biting into. Juicy peaches overflowing in baskets are handy for preparing peach ice cream and peach cobbler. One of the longest

Country-style peach cobbler. *Courtesy of DelMonte Foods, Inc.*

continuing agricultural festivals in Louisiana is the Louisiana Peach Festival, which began in 1951. Family fun, music, a peach eating contest, arts and crafts and a parade fill this annual June weekend event. "Peaches and Posies" was the first festival theme, including a flower show, peach cookery contest, art show and first crowning of the Queen Dixie Gem and Princess Peach. Dignitaries at the first event included Cajun storyteller and cookbook author Justin Wilson, who was master of ceremonies for the pageant, and Louisiana senator Dudley J. Leblanc, originator of Hadacol tonic, who presented the crown.

In 2015, the world's largest peach cobbler was prepared during the Louisiana Peach Festival in Ruston, setting a new Guinness World Record of a huge 2,251-pound fruit cobbler, which took six hours to bake. Ingredients included 819 pounds of peaches, 312 pounds of butter, 343 pounds of flour, 73 gallons of milk, 1 pound of baking powder and 454 pounds of sugar. The festival continues to entertain with a peach "everything"—treasure hunt, a messy cobbler eating contest, quilt show, parade, cookery contest and more to celebrate the cheeky peach.

HAND PIES

Sweet Dough Pie Festival (October)
Grand Coteau

The southern hand pie is the right size for a portable snack of tastiness. Whether baked or fried, the variety of hand pies may not be fancy, but they do make an imaginative use of jams, jellies and preserves. Considered an old dessert of the bayous, the sweet dough pie encouraged country folks to walk through backyard brambles to pick plump blackberries or whatever was in season. In the town of Grand Coteau, French for "big ridge," every fall for the past four years, a tart-like treat is the big attraction of the Sweet Dough Pie Festival. Visitors gather to honor the best of the best in a baking contest. Popular flavors are locally harvested, including juicy fillings of sweet potato, lemon, fig preserves, pear and blackberry. Another well-known flavor is the *tarte a la bouille*, or custard. Many home bakers use recipes handed down from their grandmothers, though their secret ingredients and techniques are closely guarded. Over one hundred booths at the festival showcase the sweet dough favorites,

A traditional treat along the bayou, the sweet dough pie. *Photo by author.*

as each booth sells an average of six hundred individual pies. Handy for freezing to use as a last-minute treat for the holidays, these pies are also the right size to pack for a picnic. The festival was created to draw people to the culture of the historic town of Grand Coteau, where more than seventy architecturally significant structures are listed in the National Register of Historic Places. Activities of the festival held on the grounds of St. Charles Borromeo Catholic Church, circa 1879, include a greedy sampling of pies as well as exploring the area through cemetery and church tours.

2439 Fairfield B&B
Shreveport

As an innkeeper in Shreveport, Jimmy Harris wears many hats. He runs the 2439 Fairfield B&B, a robin egg–blue Victorian inn of 1905 located among mansions in the Fairfield Historic District. Jimmy is also a talented chef and, most notably, an entertaining storyteller. The bed-and-breakfast was built by the Ratcliff family, and their daughter lived there

Fried hand pie prepared at the Victorian-style 2439 Fairfield Inn. *Photo by author.*

most of her life, until age ninety-three. When Jimmy purchased it in 1989, the house was in a state of disrepair. At that time, he oversaw a major renovation, installing new plumbing, adding heating and air conditioning and converting the attic to accommodate four bedroom suites. Before passing away at age ninety-nine, the original owners' daughter, Miss Irene, toured the house to look over the building improvements.

Amid the year-round collection of Santa Clauses, paperweights and a village of Christmas houses, Jimmy sets up breakfast and treats for his guests. The joyful fried hand pie is the traditional sweet he learned how to prepare from his grandmother. Each side of the half-moon pastry is lightly fried for a few minutes until it turns golden brown in color. Back home in Arkansas where he grew up, peaches and apples were ripe for picking from the family orchard from which he and Maw Maw took time to make jams and jellies. A well-worn wooden rolling pin was useful for rolling the dough to a precise thinness. Crimping the flaky pie dough to contain the delicious messiness of the fruit was the final touch.

The Kitchen Shop
296 Martin Luther King Drive
Grand Coteau

When pastry chef Nancy Brewer tasted Gateau Breton during culinary class, the sensation of the rich dessert reminded her of her grandmother's sweet dough pies in Iota, Louisiana. They were prepared open faced, rather than folded over as a half-circle, using fruit picked fresh from the farm for the filling. The buttery Gateau Breton has roots in Brittany, a cultural region in northwestern France. This specialty cake dates back to 1863, when it was introduced at the Paris Exposition as *Cake Lorient*, winning first prize in the dry pastries category. The nostalgic taste inspired Nancy to develop her own sugary combination, naming her buttery dessert filled with pecans the *gateaux na-na* in honor of her grandmother, as "na-na" is a French nickname for grandmother. She also prepares open-faced little pies with fillings of pear, fig, coconut custard and tarte a la bouille. There's more fruit than crust with these enchanting

Delicious little fruit pies at the Kitchen Shop. *Photo by author.*

pies. Nancy's jam-packed specialty shop of kitchenware, cookbooks and giftware has a cozy corner to relax in while enjoying the melt-in-your mouth desserts. It's located on the main strip in Grand Coteau near the famous oak-lined alley leading to the entrance of the Academy and Convent of the Sacred Heart, founded in 1821.

COCONUT CUSTARD PIE

Victor's Cafeteria
109 West Main Street
New Iberia

With a setting reminiscent of earlier times, Victor's Cafeteria attracts visitors to the charming downtown of New Iberia, recognized as the land of hot sauce, rice and sugarcane. This amusing spot is where the locals gather—just ask the Breakfast Club. So comfortable is this group of men who regularly enjoy gourmet breakfasts at Victor's that one of the customers, Mike, comes in at 5:00 a.m., taking charge to set the coffee pot brewing while waiting for his gang's entrance. The Art Deco building that houses this folksy eatery was built in the early 1900s for Pfister Jewelry Company. In 1970, the building was sold to Vernon and Beverly Victor Huckaby. Business acumen stems from Vernon, whose successful downtown five-and-dime store also fed patrons at a luncheonette counter with chief cook Beulah Shelby at the helm. When times changed and the dime store lease was lost, the Huckabys leased the Pfister building on Main Street to open Victor's Cafeteria. The business was turned over to their son Victor and his wife, Catherine, in 1984.

Victor's is open for breakfast and lunch in a diner-style setting. The original flooring, tin square ceiling and skylight give the place an old-time allure. For lunch, you may take a peek at what appeals to you as you slide your tray to make your choices, whether fried shrimp, catfish, gumbo, pork chops or other filling dishes. Desserts are first for viewing on the line where it's acceptable to select a wedge of pie or cake, change your mind and switch to a prettier one. One of the signature homemade sweets lovingly prepared by Catherine Huckaby is the coconut custard pie. There's also apple pie topped with pecans, bread pudding soaked in rich cream and crowned with meringue, cheesecakes and strawberry shortcake. Catherine notes that at one time, kids came in to sell their buckets of blackberries straight from roadside bushes for her to use in baking cobblers.

On display are posters by the late artist of *Blue Dog* fame, George Rodriguez, a native New Iberian and Catherine's first cousin. There is also a grouping of memorabilia about Dave Robicheaux, the fictional detective in New Iberian author James L. Burke's popular books. Using the backdrop of the eatery in his storyline, Burke sets his character Dave Robicheaux at Victor's enjoying a cup of strong coffee paired with a meal. Hot sauce memorabilia and other knickknacks remind you that just a few miles away in Avery Island is the Tabasco® Pepper Sauce Factory.

Coconut Custard Pie
Courtesy of Catherine Huckaby, Victor's Cafeteria

3¼ cups whole milk
¼ cup, or 4 tablespoons, unsalted butter
3 eggs
⅔ cup sugar
½ cup cornstarch
1½ teaspoons vanilla extract
½ (15-ounce) package refrigerated piecrust (1 sheet)
2 cups sweetened flaked coconut
1 (12-ounce) container frozen nondairy whipped topping, thawed
¼ cup toasted coconut

In a large saucepan, combine milk and butter and bring to a boil over medium heat. Remove from heat. In a large bowl, combine eggs, sugar, and cornstarch. Beat at medium speed with an electric mixer for 5 minutes. Add half of egg mixture to hot milk, whisking well to prevent curdling. When mixture is smooth and thick, add remainder of egg mixture, whisking well. Reduce heat to simmer and cook for 10 minutes until thickened. Remove from heat and add vanilla, stirring to mix well. Fill a large bowl with ice and add water to make an ice bath.

Transfer hot custard mixture to a stainless-steel bowl and set bowl over ice bath to cool to room temperature. Cover and refrigerator for one to two hours. Preheat oven to 425 degrees. Unroll piecrust and fit into a 10-inch deep-dish pie pan. Place a square of parchment paper or aluminum foil in center of piecrust. Fill center with pie weights, dried beans or rice.

Bake for 20 minutes or until lightly browned. Remove from oven, lift parchment paper or aluminum foil to remove pie weights and let cool. When custard mixture has cooled and thickened, add coconut, stirring to mix well. Spoon custard, stirring to mix well, then spoon into cooled piecrust. Top with whipped topping. Sprinkle with toasted coconut if desired.

VARIETY OF PIES

Lea's Lunchroom
1810 US Highway 71
Lecompte

Lea's Lunchroom is probably one of Louisiana's most famous landmark restaurants—worthy of detouring off the main highway that it runs along, I-49. A retro sign, "Pie Fixes Everything," hangs in this legendary diner, which is listed as a Louisiana Hall of Fame restaurant.

Despite the challenging times of the Great Depression, Lea Johnson opened Lea's in 1928 in the little town of Cheneyville in central Louisiana. He started out by selling only popcorn and coffee. To set up shop—as well as provide a gathering spot for a quick bite—he built an icebox and traded in a car in exchange for a counter and some stools. He hired a seventeen-year-old redheaded girl straight out of high school to manage the café and married Miss Georgie eleven years later. Credit Georgie's mother, who brought something to the humble station that changed everything—homemade pies, the type you used to see cooling off on the windowsill in country kitchens. So widespread was the acclaim for Lea's pies that while on the run from the law, outlaws Bonnie and Clyde stopped by to enjoy a slice of the famous pie. (Bonnie and Clyde were killed in a police ambush in Arcadia, Louisiana, in 1934.)

Years later, in 1950, Lea's moved to a larger building six miles away in the town of Lecompte. The building was also a gas station, though it was converted to a café.

Lea's daughter Ann remarks that the office where she currently conducts daily business was formerly used as her bedroom while she was

Chocolate pie at Lea's Lunchroom, a landmark restaurant in central Louisiana since 1928. *Photo by author.*

growing up, as at one time, the family lived in an apartment attached to the lunchroom. The success of the business stems from Lea and Georgie's work, and it has always been a family affair, starting with family recipes of flaky crusts and enticing fillings. Ann is just as comfortable working behind the counter as she is joining the pie makers and early risers in the kitchen and knows how to bake the pies. Nine different pies are prepared daily. A second location of Lea's was opened a few years ago in Monroe, Louisiana, by Ann's son Toby Traylor.

You can order tasty pie by the slice or take a whole pie to go. Feast your eyes on everything from meringues (chocolate, lemon, coconut or banana) to fruit (apple or peach) to berry (blueberry or cherry). Bestsellers are pecan, followed by the coconut meringue pie. There are also seasonal pies like sweet potato and pumpkin, with Thanksgiving and Christmas as the busiest times of the year. They also have a large pecan pie mailing business year-round.

Lea's is a countryside place with shelves of colorful doo-dads, displays of honey, mayhaw jelly, sunbonnets and rustic artwork for sale amid ceiling fans humming and small-town chatting. A breakfast of big southern biscuits and eggs with strong coffee and lunch are served as a build-up to the pie. There's no set menu for lunchtime chow down, as the choices are written up daily on hanging chalkboards. Lea's perfected farm-to-table concept before the culinary term became popular, as entrée selection depends on what the local farmers harvest. Three choices of meat and locally raised vegetables are available, though Lea's is acclaimed for its ham sandwiches.

Word-of-mouth descriptions of the famous pies led to an appearance for Lea Johnson in 1989 on the *Johnny Carson Tonight Show* on Thanksgiving Day. What a rascal Lea was by keeping Johnny in stitches with his ramblings about pies and life in Louisiana. He liked talking about politics and sharing a bit of local gossip. As he explained to Johnny Carson, the secret of his success was "I love people. If you love people, you're going to give them the best. Also, we don't serve riff raff around here. Nice people are always seeking a nice place to eat." Lea Johnson died in 1995 at age ninety-eight.

To honor Lea's, the Louisiana legislature declared the town of Lecompte "Pie Capital of Louisiana." The town now hosts an annual pie festival in October.

As a haven for weary travelers, Lea's Lunchroom continues to dish up a slice of old-fashioned southern hospitality.

10

Sweet Breads

CHIX-DE-FEMME

Bertinot's Best Bakery
996 West Tunnel Boulevard
Houma

The unique sweet roll from a one-hundred-year French recipe steals the show at Bertinot's Best Bakery, established in 1943. The *chix-de-femme*, French for the "bun of a woman," is a yellow spiraled pastry covered lightly with cinnamon sugar and a gooey glaze. Similar to a honey bun, the recipe for the plump roll resembling a woman's chignon is believed to have journeyed from France to Cajun Country to Excelsior Bakery, a downtown shop in Houma opened in 1880.

From here, the sojourn of the tasty treat gets a little fuzzy, as the bakery changed hands and bakers moved around while also guarding the old recipe. It ended up at Bertinot's Best Bakery in Houma, an old-fashioned shop that continues to bake fourteen dozen chix-de-femme daily, keeping the time-honored sweet before customers.

The bakers use this same classic dough to prepare their version of another Louisiana specialty, the king cake. The most requested king cake flavor is the chix-de-femme king cake, which includes pineapple bits. All

Chix-de-femme pastry, a cinnamon specialty prepared from a one-hundred-year-old recipe by Bertinot's Best Bakery in Houma. *Photo by author.*

flavors of king cake—including unique ones like Almond Joy and piña colada—are available year-round and may be decorated for any holiday or special occasion.

Pretty baked goods in a glass showcase greet customers to the cozy shop. On hand are cookies, banana and cranberry loaves, brownies, scones, mini pecan pies and bread pudding squares. The ginger cakes, with a taste similar to gingerbread, are hand rolled, and big cookie cutters are used to get a consistent oblong shape of six inches long. Another popular treat is the thin French puff pastry lightly dusted with sugar, nicknamed a "shoe sole" because of its shape.

Bertinot's pastry crew comes in at 10:00 p.m. to work all night, and the bread crew reports for duty at 3:00 a.m., all with a checklist of special orders. One hundred loaves of crusty French bread are baked daily for local restaurants, as well as for patrons waiting in line for the first hot one out of the oven. By dawn, coffee is brewing, and the lovely scent of baking is drifting throughout the neighborhood.

Anthony Matrana drove a bread truck for many years, making deliveries and taking orders, followed by years kneading dough at Best Bakery before purchasing it for his family in 1995. His daughter Melissa Bertinot was a shoe-in for taking over the shop. During her senior year in high school, her interest in the culinary field shined through upon winning first place in a baking competition in which she baked a batch of oatmeal cookies and decorated a cake. Upon graduation, Melissa was offered a scholarship to attend culinary school, yet she opted instead to arm herself with a rolling pin to begin working in the family bakery. She took over ownership ten years ago, updating the name to Bertinot's Best Bakery knowing that owning a bakeshop would mean challenges of early mornings and the tempting aroma of sweets baking all day long. But along with that came the reward of welcoming new customers overjoyed to grab a batch of yummy delights to take home.

BREAD PUDDING

Bread pudding is no wallflower dessert. Although it's considered a simple dessert that is at ease being served in fine dining cafés or small coffee shops, this sweet dish evolved from a creative manner for thrifty Cajuns and Creoles to use stale bread. It is embraced as one of the most popular desserts in Louisiana. With a clever sleight of hand, the cook may prepare bread pudding as a true custard-like pudding or more cake-like, perhaps with a meringue or rum sauce to dress it up. It's not an exotic dish, though variations are virtually endless, as the mainstay ingredients may include crusty French bread, sliced loaf bread, cinnamon raisin rolls and even doughnuts. For sweetening, honey or brown sugar, berries, fruit, chocolate, canned fruit cocktail or nuts can be added, along with a sprinkling of cinnamon and nutmeg. The layers of bread are converted to a blissful creation by thoroughly soaking them overnight in an egg and sugared milk mixture, perchance with a gentle lacing of brandy or vanilla flavoring. Once baked, the pudding is delicious served either warm or cold.

Bread pudding has been traced to late medieval times as a way to use leftover bread from feasts rather than throw it out, although it could have been prepared either sweet with rosewater rather than milk as an ingredient, or savory, stuffed with meat.

As a show of southern hospitality, a feast for guests was prepared after gentlemen spent a day out hunting and the ladies played parlor games.

Bread pudding is a delicious way to use leftover bread. *Courtesy of the Lake Charles Convention & Visitors Bureau.*

A typical antebellum evening spread included beefsteak pie, pork sausage, pickled oysters and fried chicken, along with homegrown side dishes of carrots, okra and stewed pumpkin and accompanied with sweet potato buns. Sips of molasses beer were offered to the gentlemen and raspberry cordials to the ladies. A popular dessert was sippet pudding, a forerunner to our bread pudding (sippet means a small piece of bread), as popularized in what is considered America's first regional cookbook. Homemaker Mary Randolph, a cousin of President Thomas Jefferson, published *Virginia House-Wife* in 1824, including numerous recipes of the day, as well as insight into the antebellum social culture. Her sippet pudding recipe included setting up a layer of bread slices that were enhanced with currants or raisins and dabs of butter. A mix of eggs, milk, sugar and nutmeg was poured over the layers, followed by baking. Her version advised enjoying the pudding with wine sauce.

Today's bread pudding was also known as "poor man's pudding," considered a simple dessert the lower class could enjoy. During the American Civil War, soldiers looking for something sweet used crushed crackers if they did not have bread and added a touch of sugar or honey along with some hot water or milk to fashion something similar to bread pudding.

Pujo Street Café
901 Ryan Street
Lake Charles

The quaint café in a classic red-brick building in downtown Lake Charles has an upbeat vibe. Diners may enjoy a nice stroll from the eatery to nearby art galleries as well as to the summer evening concert series "Downtown at Sundown." The building that houses the café was originally Gordon's Drug Store, built in 1886, which included a downstairs pharmacy and an upstairs doctor's office. At the time the building was constructed, Lake Charles enjoyed a growth spurt sparked largely by a regional expansion of the timber industry. As prosperity increased in the flourishing town, carriages replaced ox carts, residents flocked to Fricke's New Opera House and maskers attended fanciful Mardi Gras celebrations. A few years later, in a remodeling effort that likely gave Gordon's a second life, brick was added to the drugstore's wooden structure, which saved it from destruction during the Great Fire of 1910. The fire spread throughout the downtown area, destroying most of Lake Charles and leaving five thousand people homeless.

In 1993, Pujo Street Café opened in a terra cotta–colored house, later expanding and moving to its current location in the Gordon building. Pet-friendly courtyard dining and a rustic interior of brick, along with a woodsy bar for gathering, gives the restaurant a relaxed setting. The menu includes a nice variety of hamburgers, steak, sandwiches and seafood. Sunday brunch draws in lots of folks and so does the dreamy signature dessert of bread pudding, a custard baked to a golden brown and topped with rum sauce.

A-Bear's Café
809 Bayou Black Drive
Houma

Grab a rocking chair on the front porch to settle in at a restaurant reminiscent of grandma's kitchen. "Hebert" is a Cajun-French surname popular in these parts, though you may not be guess that the name is actually pronounced "A-Bear," and that's where the name of this family-owned restaurant originated.

Curly and Jane Hebert set up shop in 1963 with the motto "Thank you for coming to our house." While Albert "Curly" Hebert did most of the "pot cooking" like gumbo and red beans and rice from his home kitchen, he had already earned a reputation as a top hotplate lunch cook in southwest Louisiana. Jane tackled the famed homemade desserts of which she prepares six or seven daily. Most of her recipes came from her mother, Lottie Breaux, born Charlotte McGowan, who came to Louisiana from New York City in 1907 on the Orphan Train.

Originally built as a house with 1920 cypress wood, the café enjoys a country-chic atmosphere. The decoration of floral tablecloths adds to the homespun atmosphere, especially with a setup of home-canned fig preserves for sale at checkout. You'll learn a lot if you strike up a conversation with the A-Bear team, all jacks of all trades, as they rush through spending time in the kitchen preparing desserts, greeting and visiting with customers or clearing dining tables.

On the menu is local Cajun fare like gumbo, po' boys, jambalaya, fried seafood and hefty lunchtime plate lunches (well known for fried catfish). The sweet course is not something you should skip. A-Bear's is best known

Homemade desserts paired with Cajun music at A-Bear's Café in Houma. *Photo by author.*

for its luscious bread pudding, a cake-like wonder covered in warmed-up creamy sauce. Other desserts include peanut butter pie in a crunchy pie crust crowned with whipped topping, seasonal blackberry or peach cobbler, chocolate cream pie and lemon meringue pie. It's worthwhile taking an extra helping of dessert home in a to-go box for late-night snacking.

Every Friday night stands for amusing entertainment by taking in the whole experience of people-watching and listening to toe-tapping music. Lots of family and friends ramble in to sit at their usual spots. Things get hopping when the three-man band plays old Cajun-French standards like "Jolie Blonde" but with an unexpected German oompah beat from the accordion player. A catchy rendition of Hank Williams's hit "Jambalaya" includes a saxophone playing in the background. Snappy music gets dancers out to two-step as they circle around the tables. The versatile repertoire includes some Fats Domino and a Beatles tune customers can sing along with. With a cold beer in hand, foodies will enjoy the weekly *fais-do-do* (Cajun dance).

Note: Curly Hebert died in January 2017, but the legacy of his homegrown dishes lives on.

The Grapevine Café
211 Railroad Avenue
Donaldsonville

A walk through Donaldsonville's streets takes you to shotgun houses, historic churches, museums and other architectural buildings reminiscent of New Orleans. One former speak-easy called the Tavern, reportedly frequented by Al Capone during bootlegging years, now houses Grapevine Café and Gallery. The two-story building, which dates to 1925, has had an appealing charm in downtown Donaldsonville since opening its doors as a restaurant in 2001. Since major renovation was done to preserve the eatery to National Historic Preservation guidelines, it serves as a proper destination for history buffs.

A blast of color comes from local art displayed on interior brick walls overlooking original hand-crafted mosaic tiles. Live music is played on weekends in the outdoor courtyard. The setting is reminiscent of the time when a Tin Lizzie from the Roaring Twenties would drive up. The locale has been the scene of many movies, including *All the King's Men* (2006), with Sean Penn, Kate Winslet and Anthony Hopkins.

Chocolate adds some dazzle to any dish, so customers are invited to linger for the specialty of the Grapevine's luscious, award-winning white chocolate bread pudding, which is rich and creamy, doused in a white chocolate sauce. Cajun and Creole dishes are featured, including turtle soup, pecan-crusted shrimp and a multilayer specialty called Eggs-Plant Marcello, fried eggplant wheels topped with crawfish étouffée or crabmeat au gratin and poached or scrambled eggs.

Mulate's Restaurant
201 Julia Street
New Orleans

As the "Original Cajun Restaurant," Mulate's has the fun-loving mood of Mardi Gras and other entertaining aspects of New Orleans. Lively Cajun music with the fiddle and accordion, often called "chank-a-chank," is featured daily. Spontaneous entertainment is enjoyed as animated dancers twirl around the dance floor. Mulate's started as a humble eatery in the small town of Breaux Bridge, Crawfish Capital of the World, in 1980. Ten years later, Mulate's opened another location in a prime spot in New Orleans—the revitalized warehouse district. Directly across from the Ernest Morial Convention Center and the Riverwalk, the nineteenth-century building that houses Mulate's has gone through many lives as a hotel, a stable for the Faubacher Brewery, a cotton warehouse and an icehouse. Patrons recognize it as the place to go for seafood—like gumbo, crawfish, po' boys, fried alligator and frog legs for appetizers. The one-of-a-kind zydeco salad is topped with blackened catfish, grilled shrimp, fried crawfish and smoked sausage medallions. Desserts include the homemade bread pudding topped with a butter rum sauce in a recipe that includes hamburger buns. There's also key lime pie and a refreshing spiced root beer float with ice cream and spiced rum.

Mulate's Homemade Bread Pudding
Courtesy of Mulate's Restaurant, New Orleans, Louisiana

6 eggs
1 teaspoon vanilla
2 cups whole milk
2 cups half-and-half
1 cup sugar
6 hamburger buns
½ cup raisins

Preheat oven to 350 degrees. In a large bowl, whip eggs, and then add vanilla, milk, and half-and-half. Mix well. Add sugar and mix well. Grease a 9 x 13 pan. Break hamburger buns into pieces and place in greased pan. Sprinkle raisins evenly throughout the bun pieces. Pour egg mixture over buns. Using your fingers, make sure that all bun pieces are soaked with the mixture. Bake for approximately 45 minutes. If you prefer a firmer texture, chill for about 2 hours, then reheat for serving.

Butter Rum Sauce

½ stick butter
¼ cup sugar

½ cup half-and-half (or heavy cream)
½ cup rum

Melt butter. Add sugar and cook on medium heat for 3 minutes. Add half-and-half and rum and cook for 5 more minutes or until slightly thickened. Serve warm over bread pudding. Serves 8 to 10.

FRENCH TOAST

Pain Perdu / Lost Bread

The crispy fried breads we know as French toast are a simple dish with a regal history. During the days of the Roman Empire, it was called *pan dulcis*, and Romans soaked bread slices in a milk and egg mixture before frying them in oil or butter. In Britain, one version was called "Poor Knights of Windsor," though the boozy bread was dipped in a beaten egg yolk followed by a soaking in a sugar and sherry mixture before frying. The Poor Knights of Windsor was a military order formed by King Edward III in the fourteenth century. French toast was also known in Britain as *gilden sippets*, which were bread slices sprinkled with rosewater. It is known as rascal's slice in Switzerland and bread-in-a-coat in the Czech Republic.

In Louisiana, we know it more as a custardy affair. As Creoles never wasted anything, the sweet dish became a good way to rescue bread, especially crusty New Orleans French bread that can become stale overnight. As a breakfast treat or a nice dessert, the bread slices are soaked in an egg, sugar and milk mixture with a dab of vanilla flavoring, sometimes with a little cinnamon or nutmeg thrown in. Then the slices are lightly pan fried in butter until golden brown on both sides. Dressing it up with berries or cut-up fruit, spooning on top a dollop of jam, drizzling with Louisiana sugar cane syrup or sprinkling with powdered sugar adds to the flavor.

Elizabeth's Restaurant
601 Gallier Street
New Orleans

It takes some imagination to combine the two well-known Louisiana standards of pain perdu and flaming Bananas Foster to make one killer breakfast treat: overstuffed Bananas Foster French Toast. But Chef Byron Peck's dressed-up version magically ties in the flamboyance of bananas but without the flame. Puffy slices of French bread are lightly grilled and stuffed with delicious Bananas Foster cream cheese.

A hipster joint, Elizabeth's Restaurant is located in a one-hundred-year-old building that was formerly a corner grocery store. Located in the artsy ByWater neighborhood of New Orleans among a bohemian gathering of Creole cottages and shotgun houses, the eatery is a shining star.

Crowds have flocked to this funky restaurant for its popular weekend brunch since 1996, singing high praise for the eclectic menu. It's a bustling, two-storied place with a ramshackle charm, decorated with colorful artwork

Elizabeth's, a funky eatery in the ByWater neighborhood of New Orleans. *Photo by author.*

Whatever you may call it—pain perdu, lost bread or French toast—it's a tasty dessert or breakfast treat. *Courtesy of Elizabeth's Restaurant.*

and bright tablecloths. Appropriately, piggy décor abounds, as Elizabeth's features praline bacon, a startling combo of pecan candy and salty pork the restaurant introduced twenty years ago. Aside from the overstuffed Bananas Foster French Toast, other dreamy desserts are on the menu, like the lemon chess pie and red velvet cake.

Another brunch/dessert special is New Orleans calas cakes, a fried rice ball similar to beignets, topped with powdered sugar and dipped in Louisiana cane syrup.

"Real Food, Done Real Good" is what Elizabeth's offers for breakfast, weekend brunch, lunch and dinner. It's a fun place to hang out while sampling unique dishes, and there's also a bar upstairs.

Old Castillo Hotel
220 Evangeline Boulevard
St. Martinville

Perhaps it was kismet when Louisiana native Peggy Hulin considered buying the Old Castillo Hotel, which began life in 1829 as steamboat captain Edmond Castillo's luxurious inn for steamboat travelers along the Bayou Teche in St. Martinville. During the nineteenth century, St. Martinville was nicknamed "Le Petit Paris," Louisiana's third-oldest city. It was a fashionable resort that attracted New Orleans residents seeking a romantic getaway. The city is blessed with a rich and romantic history tied to a story of lost lovers through poet Henry Wadsworth Longfellow's 1847 story of Acadian lovers Evangeline and Gabriel. Separated during the Acadian exile from Canada, Evangeline died of a broken heart beneath the moss-laden branches of the Evangeline Oak, which now provides shading for the Old Castillo Hotel.

When steamboat travel gave way to railroads, the hotel was sold to the Sisters of Mercy, who operated it as a convent and boarding school for girls for over one hundred years. Current innkeeper Peggy Hulin had no experience in running a restaurant or a bed-and-breakfast. While

Romantic setting of the Old Castillo Hotel in St. Martinville. *Photo by author.*

researching the history of the Castillo Hotel site, one of her cousins relayed that one of their direct ancestors, Don Louis Broussard, had once actually owned the property. Peggy took this as a sure sign to move forward with her plans of purchasing the building in 1987. She ran it first as a restaurant and now as a three-storied bed-and-breakfast with seven guest rooms.

French toast is served as part of the Cajun breakfast for her guests. An old family recipe uses stale sliced bread (she bakes her own bread) soaked in a mix of sugar, eggs and vanilla. She calls it lost bread, or in French, *pain perdu*, and explains to visitors, many who are new to Louisiana, why it's called this as an introduction to the Cajun culture. People routinely baked their own bread before the days they could buy it wrapped on the store shelf. After a few days, the bread became stale and would be lost, or wasted, so making lost bread was a good way to prepare something special.

Bistro Byronz
8200 Village Plaza Court
Baton Rouge

Ooh la la! With an appealing décor, mostly in rich wood and black-and-white accents, this southern version of a quaint neighborhood French café has a full menu for brunch, lunch and dinner. Aside from soups and salads, there's an outlandish sandwich called "gumbo po' boy" of chicken and sausage gumbo served on po' boy bread. Food Network's show *Burgers, Brew & Que* praised the Bistro for its croque madame hamburger, which features a slab of griddled ham and a poached egg stacked on a ground turkey patty that is drenched in a bacony Mornay sauce. Originally an unpretentious mom-and-pop sandwich shop called Byronz in 1980, the bistro was resurrected in 2005 when the Kantrow family reopened it as Bistro Byronz with a French flair, offering a wider selection of dishes. Whether sampling eggs or shrimp and grits for brunch, diners also enjoy the impressive pain perdu. The bistro makes its own signature bread, and once slightly stale, the slices are dipped into an egg and milk batter and then cooked on a flattop griddle until golden brown on both sides. It's dusted with powdered sugar and served with a homemade blackberry merlot sauce for dipping. For lunch, the key lime pie for dessert hits the spot. Bistro Byronz has a second Baton Rouge location on Government Street, which was its first site, and other locations in Mandeville and Shreveport.

MONKEY BREAD

Monkey bread is a pull-apart bread that bears a silly name derived from the baked bread's resemblance to a barrel of monkeys. Though the story of the amusing bread flows like a tall tale, monkey bread was popularized in Southern California in the 1940s by silent movie actress ZaSu Pitts, who had a passion for baking. Aside from starring in movies, she actually took her culinary hobby seriously by writing a confectionery cookbook, published posthumously in 1963. During her role in a movie called *Ramshackle Inn*, ZaSu was introduced to fellow actress Nancy Davis. Nancy Davis became Nancy Reagan when she married fellow actor Ronald Reagan, who later became America's fortieth president.

During the early 1970s, the Reagans bought a California ranch and were reintroduced to the delicious monkey bread at one of the local bakeries. After Reagan was inaugurated president in 1981, the First Lady, who had always prized the special treat of monkey bread, began a Christmas tradition in the White House by serving it to family and friends.

Earlier variations of the whimsical dish was called jumble loaf or bubble bread. Basically, it consists of dough balls made from scratch or from cut-up

First Lady Nancy Reagan in the White House kitchen. Monkey bread was served at the White House during Christmas events. *Courtesy of Ronald Reagan Presidential Library.*

canned biscuit dough that are dipped in butter and placed snuggled up style in a cake pan with a hole in the middle to ensure even baking. The balls are layered on top of one another while a variety of frills such as cinnamon sugar, chopped nuts, chopped fruit, jam or chocolate syrup drizzle may be added. The ring of delight is baked until lightly browned and the rolls can be pulled out.

Nancy Reagan's Monkey Bread

6 ounces butter, softened
4½ cups all-purpose flour
1 package active dry yeast
1 cup lukewarm milk
3 large eggs
3 tablespoons sugar
1 teaspoon salt
4 ounces melted butter

Butter and flour a nine-inch mold or bundt pan and set aside. Whisk the yeast with the milk in a large bowl. Whisk in two of the eggs, then add dry ingredients of sugar, salt and four cups of flour. Switch to a spoon when the dough gets stiff. Cut in softened butter and knead the dough in the bowl until it comes together in a ball. Turn out onto lightly floured work area, continuing to knead to keep dough from getting sticky by adding the remaining ½ cup of flour. Place dough in a clean bowl and cover with plastic wrap. Let rise in a warm place for 1 to 1½ hours, until doubled in size.

Return dough to a lightly floured work area and punch it down. Roll dough into a log shape and cut into twenty-eight equal-size pieces. Roll each piece into a ball, dip in melted butter and place in prepared pan, staggering pieces in two layers. Cover loosely with plastic wrap and let rise in a warm place until doubled, about 30 minutes. Preheat oven to 375 degrees. Beat remaining egg and lightly brush the top layer. Bake until top is nicely browned, 25 to 30 minutes. Cool on a rack before sliding out the loaf for serving. For variations, coat the balls in cinnamon and brown sugar. Once baked and cooled, drizzle with cream cheese or jam glaze.

Great Harvest of Acadiana
854A Kaliste Saloom Road
Lafayette

Operating a family-owned bakery in Lafayette in its eleventh year, owners J.P. and his wife, Michelle MacFadyen, incorporate baking both sweet and savory masterpieces every morning. To prepare their version of monkey bread, which J.P. knew as pull-apart bread in his native Pennsylvania, they use surplus cinnamon rolls. The bread is baked and served in a pie pan. Once baked, the round loaf is flipped over and embellished with a special topping of smooth golden honey, pecans and cinnamon sugar.

After spending time in Colorado, the MacFadyens returned to Michelle's native Louisiana. They began the business of grinding wheat and baking bread made from scratch by opening Great Harvest. Restocking bounty on the shelves, brewing coffee all day, offering samples—these are duties the MacFadyen children have been assigned

The jumbled-up sweet known as monkey bread. *Photo by author.*

at the shop since an early age, including setting out tasty treats every Saturday at the local farmers' market.

The specialty bakery is committed to being involved in the community. For Father's Day, the owners host a hands-on baking session for kids to prepare special cookies for their dads. Getting into the spirit during carnival season, gold, purple and green sugars are sprinkled over their king cake. During a recent flood, the bakery prepared hundreds of trays of treats to serve at local shelters for those displaced from home.

A variety of sandwiches is available for lunch featuring Great Harvest's hot cross buns, Irish soda bread, sundried tomato bread and walnut fig bread. The oven works nonstop, cranking up before sunrise, slowly turning like a Ferris wheel as rotating trays accommodate a wide variety of breads at a count of three hundred loaves at a time. Their bestsellers are cinnamon burst extreme bread and pepperoni bread. For sweets, they bake muffins, s'mores bars with toasted marshmallows, scones, bread pudding squares, cinnamon rolls as big as the moon, white chocolate berry swirl bread and pumpkin bread. Their version of a holiday fruitcake, called Kentucky Bourbon Bread, includes bourbon-soaked figs, apricots and raisins. The dried fruit is mixed with Louisiana pecans and walnuts and 100 percent whole wheat flour. The bakery's mission is to incorporate ingredients like honey and produce such as strawberries and figs from local growers and suppliers. There's lots of down-to-earth originality in making their delicious range of specialty bakery treats.

11

Sweet Taters

*C*onsidered a southern staple because it thrives in a warm climate, the coppery sweet potato is a root vegetable that belongs to the morning glory flower family. The names of sweet potato and its comrade in arms, the yam, are often interchanged. Savvy cooks recognize that the sweet potato is handy for preparing pancakes, cakes and fries as well as the prized standard of the sweet potato pie. Trendy because of its desirability for health-conscious consumers, the sweet potato is high in beta carotene.

Sweet potatoes were grown in Peru as early as 750 BC. When Columbus sailed the ocean blue, arriving in America in 1492, Native Americans met him at the dock with many new foods, including the treasured sweet potato, so it is no wonder that it was one of the dishes served at the Pilgrims' first Thanksgiving.

Pioneering conservationist Dr. George Washington Carver (1864–1943) experimented with sweet potatoes. He encouraged farmers to plant them as crops in soil that was worn out from growing cotton. There were no barriers for his imagination intertwined with scientific reason. Ink from sweet potatoes? Carver proved the versatility of sweet potatoes by developing one hundred products from the tuber, including flour, ink, starch, molasses, vinegar, paints and glue for postage stamps. His experiments carried over to the kitchen, as Dr. Carver came up with and promoted his own recipe for sweet potato pie.

Sweet potato pie. *Courtesy of the Louisiana Sweet Potato Commission.*

Anna's Old-Fashioned Pies
2323 Moeling Street
Lake Charles

Her sweet potato pies and gingerbread are great. But the sweet potato cake may send you over the edge. When you embrace Miss Anna, the creator of all of this goodness, you also hug whiffs of cinnamon and a little nutmeg. There's always a mountain of mashed sweet potatoes in the shop, ready to use in preparation of her homemade cakes and pies, which are her pride and joy.

Over twenty years ago, Anna Manuel, from the rural community of Lawtell in St. Landry Parish, faced a health setback. She suffered with rheumatoid arthritis, limiting her capability for working. While searching in her home cupboard for her mother's pie dough recipe, she recognized that baking was something she could continue to do, even though for a period she was in a wheelchair. Growing up around fields of sweet potatoes on her father's farm, Anna recalls digging them from rows. The family also had fig trees and apple trees. "Back then, you had to load up the fruit in baskets and slice it in preparation for cooking preserves to use in baking," Anna noted. "We also had sugar cane and made syrup to bake gateau de sirop [syrup cake]."

With a lone rolling pin on hand, she began her venture by baking a few pies to sell to family members. This grew to selling to neighborhood grocery stores. Humbly packaged, the heavenly pies and cakes are now distributed to gas stations and grocery stores along the Gulf Coast from Houston to Biloxi. Her selection of sweets can also be found in coffee and gift shops in the French Quarter and many casinos. Or stop by Anna's shop in Lake Charles to stock up.

It's still mostly a cottage business, with the majority of the work being done by hand to ensure the quality of the forty products Anna produces. Over three thousand pies are baked daily, and keeping up with larger numbers during the holiday season keeps the shop busy.

Her bestseller is the sweet potato pie. These are prepared in a nice, individual size where you won't have to share because honestly you don't want to share this down-to-earth sweet treat. Larger pies like pecan, cherry and peach (some with lattice) are also baked, as well as gingerbread planks, strawberry cakes and rum cakes by special request.

Anna's Pies won the Lantern Award for Louisiana businesses under Governor Kathleen Blanco in 2005 in recognition for excellence in manufacturing and contributing to the local community.

Take a wild guess who's most popular at Miss Anna's family reunions? Hint: she always brings desserts!

Yam Country Pies
430 East Grolee Street
Opelousas

The city of Opelousas, founded in 1720, was recognized early on for agricultural cultivation, leading up to its distinction as the Yam Capital of the World with an accompanying celebration. At its height, the Opelousas Yambilee, a festival of agricultural competition, beauty queens and parades, drew politicians such as John F. Kennedy when he was a Massachusetts senator. The sweet potato—which has been on the rise as a healthy option, prepared candied, as fries, medallions or in a soufflé—has been enjoyed in Louisiana from the time French settlers established Opelousas as a trading post.

It's in this setting that Yam Country Pies began baking sweet treats from fifty years of "made from scratch" experience.

At seventy-five years old, Patricia Hertzock wanted to preserve and share her family's tradition of baking sweet dough pies. Years earlier, several of her great aunts baked pies and fried doughnuts for Holy Ghost Catholic Church functions. But it was her mother's love of baking to perfection that inspired and guided her to pass on the skills and talents to her children and grandchildren.

Upon retiring as a school librarian, the last thing Patricia planned for her golden years was to launch a business. But when she participated in Grand Coteau's Sweet Dough Pie contest and walked away with a blue ribbon, an idea was kicked off to begin baking these handsome, five-inch folded pies. She started by baking a few pies from her own kitchen for special orders.

Yam Country Pies opened in 2011 in a small building on South Union Street before moving to a new location in the historic district of Opelousas in a former 1930s country store. The original shopkeeper's family had living quarters in the back, which has proven useful for all of the mixing, baking and planning that takes place to produce five trays of pies at sixteen pies per tray, baking fifteen minutes in the oven. Patricia still makes good display use of the country store's original wooden shelving, which once housed canned goods. The shop also prepares full-size latticed pies and tea cakes. These little round tea cakes, about the size of a vanilla wafer, use the sweet dough recipe but without any filling.

The dough is similar to that of a pie crust, but as the name implies, there is a tender bit of sweetness in it. Small bits of dough are shaped in a circle, stuffed with filling, folded over and crimped shut. The dough is prepared a day or so in advance to allow for rising. The number-one seller is the sweet potato pie, but Yam Country Pies also bakes peach, fig, pumpkin, apple and a few others. The business reaches out to local farmers to provide the fruit. It's the romantic scent of baking, especially the nutmeg, that lets the neighborhood know that the pies are ready. Patricia calls it "Love at First Bite." Each batch gets every family member involved—promoting, sampling, cleaning up, measuring ingredients or buying supplies to ensure a flavorful reward.

Sweet Potato Praline Brownies
Courtesy of Louisiana Sweet Potato Commission

1 large sweet potato
5 large egg whites
1 cup softened unsalted butter, divided
1 cup sugar
½ cup unsweetened cocoa powder
½ teaspoon baking powder
2 teaspoons vanilla extract, divided
1½ cups chopped pecans, divided
1 cup brown sugar
¼ teaspoon of salt
½ cup evaporated milk
½ cup confectioners sugar

Prick sweet potato all over with a fork. Wrap in a wet paper towel and microwave on high heat for 5 minutes. Continue to microwave in 2-minute intervals until soft. Set aside to cool. Once potato is cool, peel, mash and reserve pulp. Preheat oven to 350 degrees. Lightly grease an 8-inch square baking pan. In a large bowl, beat egg whites at high speed with an electric mixer until stiff peaks form. In the bowl of a stand mixer, combine ½ cup butter and sugar. Using the paddle attachment, beat at medium speed until combined.

Add cocoa powder, baking powder and 1 teaspoon vanilla. Gently fold in egg whites to combine. Stir in ½ cup pecans and sweet potato. Transfer to prepared pan and bake 25 to 30 minutes or until center is firm. In a heavy saucepan, melt ½ cup butter over medium heat. Add brown sugar and salt, and bring to a boil. Cook for 2 minutes, stirring constantly. Remove from heat and slowly whisk in evaporated milk. Return saucepan to stove and bring mixture to a boil again. Boil, stirring constantly, until mixture reaches 230° on a candy thermometer (soft ball stage). Remove from heat, and stir for 2 minutes; let cool to lukewarm. Add remaining 1 teaspoon vanilla and confectioner's sugar. Stir until combined. Pour mixture over warm brownies and top with remaining 1 cup pecans. Let cool to room temperature before cutting. Makes 1½ dozen.

12

Coffee and Sweets

La gregue est chaude is a common front porch expression that literally means "the coffeepot is hot" in French. But what it means between-the-lines among neighbors can be understood as "Come in cher, let's visit. Tell me the news. *Tu va bien?* (Are you good?). I'll make a pot of coffee and cut a slice of upside cake that I baked yesterday. Maybe we'll have a joke or two to share."

Along the bayous, drinking strong Louisiana coffee was part of rural life. Sharing cups of coffee became a way to seal a friendship among neighbors. Farmers were up when the rooster crowed, and the smell of coffee brewing in the kitchen filled the house. The habit of drinking coffee along with swallowing a slice of honey cornbread for breakfast helped the hardworking farmer wake up and gave him a boost to face working in the field. Quilting bees encouraged ladies to visit while the hostess set up a tray of pecan pie in wintertime or blackberry tarts in the spring, along with a dainty demitasse of coffee. There was great stock placed in the trusted French drip coffee pot. On many mornings, kids were treated to pain perdu (French toast) topped off with cut-up berries alongside a cup of café au lait (coffee milk) before walking to school.

The pairing of coffee and sweet tidbits was a match made in heaven, having been part of the Louisiana culture for over two hundred years when coffee first arrived in the major port of New Orleans, primarily from Latin American coffee planters. The first coffee stand in New Orleans is credited to former slave Rose Nicaud, who set up her own simple station, bravely

Pineapple upside-down cake. *Courtesy of DelMonte Foods Inc.*

setting an example for other free women of color to open their own stands by selling café noir or café au lait near the French Market. There was a growth spurt of five hundred coffeehouses, called exchange houses, opening in New Orleans and frequented largely by businessmen by the mid-1800s due to the popularity of the hot brew. Today, New Orleans is America's premier coffee handling port.

The evolution from coffee to café au lait stems from a disrupted delivery of coffee and other popular commodities. During the American Civil War, Union naval blockades cut off the port of New Orleans, leading resourceful Louisianians to develop an additive to their much-loved coffee to stretch the supply. Various experiments were conducted by drying and roasting acorns, peanuts, okra seeds and beets, with the most satisfactory filler being chicory. This root of the endive plant does not contain caffeine. When roasted and ground, chicory adds an unmistakable nutty taste to the coffee and reduces bitterness. Café au lait is considered chicory coffee blended and toned down with boiled milk.

From humble beginnings to what is now the largest family-owned (now in its fourth generation) and operated retail coffee brand in America, Community Coffee remains one of the best-loved coffees in Louisiana. It began when

Cap Saurage (rhymes with "garage") opened a country store in the Dixie neighborhood of Baton Rouge in 1910, selling coffee and groceries.

As a way to keep customers loyal, the store became a gathering spot, with a fresh pot of free coffee always ready for pouring. Cap bought fresh roasted coffee beans from New Orleans, ever tweaking the blend recipe. The coffee became so admired by the store's clientele that Cap began the process of grinding and packaging the coffee himself. The coffee was scooped by the pound and packaged in brown paper sacks with a hand-stenciled mark of "Community Coffee" and delivered by horse-drawn wagons to customers. The Community brand was registered as a federal trademark in 1919. By 1923, due to the popularity of the coffee, the grocery store had closed while the backyard barn was converted into a coffee grinding mill, complete with a large grinder and packing table. By 1924, Cap Saurage and brother-in-law Albert Dupuy had taken over delivery trucks to transport their coffee to area grocery stores. As the coffee business continued to expand, efforts were devoted to mechanical advancements in grinding and scooping the special blend of roasted coffee.

A Community Coffee truck loaded with one-hundred-pound sacks of medium roast coffee, 1931. *Courtesy of Community Coffee Company.*

During the 1930s, Community Coffee entered new markets in Louisiana. A new plant was built in Baton Rouge along with a testing lab, increasing opportunities to roast their own coffee as the partners began importing Brazilian coffee beans.

Now Community Coffee is distributed throughout the southeast region of the United States. Among many accolades, Community Coffee is the official coffee of the New Orleans Saints football team.

Statistics show that 64 percent of Americans over the age of eighteen drink coffee every day. For the coffee connoisseur looking for a "cup of Joe," Community Coffee now blends several flavored coffees—chicory, pumpkin praline, southern bread pudding, pecan praline, hazelnut and French vanilla—among other varieties in single cup format.

Additional Recipes

Skinny Pumpkin Poke Cake
Courtesy of Quincy L. Cheek, home economist
LSU AgCenter, Lecompte, Louisiana

This cake can easily be converted to a Louisiana favorite by substituting 2 cups mashed sweet potatoes in the place of the pumpkin.

1 box yellow cake mix
2 cups cooked pumpkin, mashed (or one 15-ounce can of 100 percent pure pumpkin)
½ cup water
1 teaspoon pumpkin pie spice
1 (1-ounce) package of fat-free/sugar-free cheesecake pudding dessert mix
2 cups cold skim milk
1 (8-ounce) container of fat-free whipped topping
¼ cup of roasted and chopped pecans

Preheat oven to 350 degrees and lightly coat a 9- by 13-inch baking dish with cooking spray. In a large bowl, mix cake mix, pumpkin, water and pumpkin pie spice. Mix with electric mixer for 2 to 3 minutes until batter is lump-free and fluffy. Transfer batter to baking pan and bake cake for 30 to 35 minutes until edges are golden brown and toothpick inserted into center comes out clean. Allow cake to cool completely. Using the end of a wooden spoon, generously poke holes all over cake. In a medium bowl, whisk together pudding mix and skim milk for roughly 2 minutes until pudding mixture thickens. Immediately pour pudding mixture evenly over cake. Top cake with whipped topping and pecans. You may lightly sprinkle a little of the pumpkin pie spice over the dessert for a little extra garnish. Place cake in refrigerator until ready to serve. Keep leftovers in refrigerator.

Silken Chocolate Pecan Tart
Courtesy of the National Pecan Shellers Association

1 ½ cups chocolate cookie crumbs
1 ½ cups ginger cookie crumbs
¾ cup brown sugar, dark
½ cup pecan meal
4 ounces unsalted butter, melted
1 ½ cups heavy cream
½ cup whole milk
3 cups semisweet chocolate
1 egg, beaten
¼ cup pecan vodka

Place all cookie crumbs, brown sugar and pecan meal in a bowl and combine well. Add melted butter and mix well. Press crumb into a greased baking dish (9 x 13). Bake for 10 minutes at 350 degrees. Remove and cool and set aside. In a small pot, scald heavy cream and milk. Pour over semisweet chocolate (chopped chocolate or chips) and let sit for 3 minutes. Using a rubber spatula, combine the dairy and chocolate. Add one beaten egg and stir quickly to incorporate. Add pecan vodka to chocolate mixture and combine well. Pour over cooled cookie crust and bake 325 degrees for 25 to 30 minutes or until there is no "jiggle" in the center. Remove from oven and cool completely. Cover with plastic wrap. Place in refrigerator and chill 24 hours. Remove from cooler and cut into desired size.

Vintage trade card of a woman baking (1876–90). *Courtesy of the New York Public Library.*

Blueberry Lemon Parfait
Courtesy of the U.S. Highbush Blueberry Council

2¼ cups vanilla Greek-style yogurt
¾ cup lemon curd
12 gingersnap cookies, crushed
2 cups fresh blueberries

In a medium bowl combine yogurt and lemon curd. In a parfait glass, layer ¼ cup yogurt mixture, 1 heaping tablespoon cookie crumbs and 1 heaping tablespoon blueberries. Repeat. Top with ¼ cup yogurt mixture and a heaping tablespoon of blueberries. Repeat in 3 more parfait glasses. Parfaits can be chilled in the refrigerator for 1 to 2 hours before serving. Makes 4 parfaits.

Braune Kuchen (Honey Cookies)
Courtesy of Roberts Cove Germanfest Cookbook

1 ½ cups honey
1 stick margarine
1 cup firmly packed brown sugar
5¼ cups flour
1 ½ tablespoons powdered sugar
1 egg
¾ cup chopped almonds or pecans
2 tablespoons cocoa
1 teaspoon ground cinnamon
¼ teaspoon ground nutmeg
¼ teaspoon ground allspice
1 egg white, slightly beaten
Chopped almonds, chopped candied cherries or candy sprinkles
Flour

Preheat oven to 325 degrees. In a 1-quart saucepan, heat honey, margarine and brown sugar over medium heat, stirring constantly, until well blended. Remove from heat; allow to cool. Meanwhile, in a large bowl, combine flour, powdered sugar, egg, almonds, cocoa and spices. Stir in cooled honey mixture; mix until smooth and well blended. Divide dough into 3 equal parts. On a lightly floured pastry board, roll each section into a thin sheet. Use cookie cutters to cut dough. Bake on greased cookie sheets for about 10 minutes. While cookies are still warm, brush with beaten egg white. Decorate with almonds, candied cherries or candy sprinkles. Makes about 6½ dozen.

Orange Almond Honey Muffins
Courtesy of the National Honey Board

1 ¼ cups all-purpose flour
1 teaspoon baking powder
½ teaspoon baking soda
¼ teaspoon salt
¼ cup butter or margarine, softened
½ cup honey
1 egg
¼ cup orange juice concentrate
½ teaspoon grated orange peel
½ cup chopped toasted almonds

In a small bowl, combine flour, baking powder, baking soda and salt; set aside. Using an electric mixer, beat butter and honey until light. Beat in egg, orange juice concentrate and orange peel. Gradually add flour mixture, mixing until just blended; stir in almonds. Spoon into 8 greased or paper-lined 2½-inch muffin cups. Bake at 350 degrees for 25 to 30 minutes or until toothpick inserted in center comes out clean. Remove muffins from pan to wire rack. Serve warm at room temperature.

Sweet Potato Bread Pudding
Courtesy of the Houmas House Plantation

8 tablespoons butter
I loaf soft French or Italian bread, torn into large pieces
2 medium sweet potatoes
4 cups milk
4 eggs
I cup sugar
I tablespoon vanilla extract
I teaspoon ground cinnamon

Preheat oven to 400 degrees. Butter a medium baking dish with I tablespoon of the butter. Arrange bread in a single layer in the prepared dish and set aside at room temperature to dry out slightly, about 2 hours. Meanwhile, prick sweet potatoes in 4 or 5 places with the tines of a fork and bake on a baking sheet until soft, about I hour. Set aside until cool enough to handle, then halve lengthwise and scoop meat out of skins. If meat holds together, break it into large pieces. Tuck sweet potato pieces between the pieces of bread, mashing them down slightly with a fork. Beat together milk, eggs, sugar, vanilla and cinnamon in a large bowl. Pour over bread and sweet potatoes and set aside until bread soaks up milk mixture, 2 to 3 hours. Preheat oven to 375 degrees. Cut the remaining 7 tablespoons of butter into small pieces and scatter over bread pudding, then bake until custard is set, 35 to 40 minutes. Set aside to cool for at least 30 minutes before serving warm or at room temperature. Serves 12.

Sweet potato bread pudding.
Courtesy of the Houmas House Plantation.

No-Bake Chocolate Brownies
Courtesy of the National Honey Board

½ cup honey
¼ cup coconut oil
¼ cup almond butter
¼ teaspoon sea salt
1 teaspoon vanilla extract
1 teaspoon ground cinnamon
½ cup chopped almonds
½ cup chopped walnuts
½ cup semisweet chocolate chips
¼ cup sunflower seeds
¼ cup dried cranberries
1 cup rolled oats
1 tablespoon butter

In a medium-sized saucepan, heat honey, coconut oil, almond butter, sea salt, vanilla and cinnamon over low heat. Next, in a large bowl, combine chopped almonds, chopped walnuts, semisweet chocolate chips, sunflower seeds, dried cranberries and rolled oats. Add the honey mixture from the saucepan into the bowl and mix. Using your hands or a spatula, grease an 8- by 8-inch pan with the butter. Press the brownie mixture into the pan and refrigerate until hardened. Cut into 16 bars and serve.

Lurline Langlois's Pralines
Courtesy of the Houmas House Plantation

1 cup sugar
1 cup brown sugar
½ cup evaporated milk
½ cup pecans

In a small, thick-bottomed sauce pan, combine all ingredients and heat over medium high heat. Bring mixture to a boil and cook for 6 minutes or until 240 degrees, stirring constantly. Remove from heat and stir until mixture thickens, becomes creamy and pecans stay suspended in mixture. Spoon out on wax paper, aluminum foil or parchment paper. Makes 15 pralines.

Snicker Doodles
Courtesy of Mary Boudreaux, Crystal Weddings Bakery

½ cup butter
½ cup Crisco
¼ cup sugar
1 ¼ cups brown sugar
2 large eggs
2 teaspoons vanilla
3½ cup flour
2 teaspoons cream of tartar
1 teaspoon baking soda
½ teaspoon salt
¼ sugar
4 teaspoons cinnamon

Preheat oven to 350 degrees. Mix together butter, Crisco, sugar, brown sugar, eggs and vanilla in large bowl. In a separate bowl, mix flour, cream of tartar, baking soda and salt. Mix both batters together. In a third bowl, mix ¼ cup sugar and 4 teaspoons cinnamon. Roll dough into balls and roll balls into cinnamon sugar mixture and place on pan 2 inches apart. Bake for 7 to 10 minutes.

Stuffed Dates
Courtesy of Author

A Christmas favorite appetizer prepared by my mother.

2 (8-ounce) packages whole pitted dates
1 (8-ounce) package cream cheese, softened at room temperature
1 small jar of maraschino cherries
½ cup of whole pecans

Butterfly the dates to open them slightly. In a bowl, mix the cream cheese and add a few spoonfuls of cherry juice. Finely chop some of the cherries to add to the cream cheese mixture. Spread the cream cheese mix on the dates to fill. Garnish with a whole pecan or cherries. Refrigerate.

Country Apple Dessert
Courtesy of Roberts Cove Germanfest

1 box yellow cake mix
⅓ cup butter, softened
2 eggs
1 can apple pie filling
½ cup brown sugar
½ cup chopped pecans
1 teaspoon cinnamon
1 cup sour cream
1 teaspoon vanilla

Heat oven to 350 degrees. In a large bowl combine cake mix, butter and 1 egg at low speed until crumbly. Press in ungreased 13 x 9 pan. Spread pie filling over cake mixture. Combine brown sugar, nuts and cinnamon in a bowl and sprinkle over apples. In another bowl combine sour cream, 1 egg and vanilla and smooth over. Bake 40 to 50 minutes until done.

Backroads Buttermilk Fruit Tart
Courtesy of American Sugar Refining, Inc./Domino Sugar, a division of the American Sugar Refining Group (ASR)

Crust

Prepared frozen or refrigerated pastry for single crust 9-inch pie

Filling

1 cup Domino granulated sugar
½ cup unsalted butter or margarine, softened
3 eggs
¼ cup all purpose flour
¾ cup buttermilk
½ teaspoon nutmeg
3 cups assorted fresh fruit, including sliced peaches, blueberries, raspberries and strawberries

3 tablespoons apricot preserves
2 teaspoons water

Heat oven to 350 degrees. Press pastry into bottom and up sides of 9-inch tart pan. Trim edges. In a large bowl, beat sugar and butter until light and fluffy. Add eggs, one at a time, mixing well after each addition. Add flour; mix well. Add buttermilk and nutmeg; mix well. Pour mixture into pastry-lined tart pan. Bake 30 to 35 minutes or until knife inserted in center comes out clean. Cool to room temperature. Arrange fruit over cooled tart. In small bowl, combine apricot preserves and water; brush over fruit. Makes 8 servings.

Lemon Ice Box Pie
Courtesy of Mulate's, New Orleans

Crust

2 cups finely crumbled vanilla wafers
½ cup melted butter

Filling

3 egg yolks
1 can sweetened condensed milk
½ cup freshly-squeezed lemon juice
1 teaspoon finely grated lemon zest
Whipped cream

Mix crust ingredients. Line a pie pan with this mixture. Chill for 30 minutes before adding filling. Preheat oven to 300 degrees. Beat egg yolks until light and fluffy. Add condensed milk and mix well. Slowly add lemon juice (the juice "cooks" the eggs and thickens the mixture). Stir in lemon zest. Pour into prepared crust. Bake for 30 minutes. Top with whipped cream if desired.

Gateau de Sirop with Chocolate
Courtesy of Author

Syrup cake is an old Cajun dessert that was very popular during sugar shortages of the Great Depression and wartime. Here is a variation of the old favorite.

2½ cups sifted all-purpose flour
1 teaspoon ground cinnamon
1 teaspoon ground ginger
½ teaspoon salt
¾ cup Enjoy Life semisweet mini chocolate baking chips
½ cup vegetable oil
1½ cups Steen's Cane Syrup
2 tablespoons honey
1 egg
1½ teaspoons baking soda
½ cup hot water
½ cup chopped pecans or walnuts, optional

In one bowl, mix flour, cinnamon, ginger and salt. Stir with fork to mix well. In a separate bowl, melt the mini chips in a microwave for 1½ minutes then combine vegetable oil, syrup, honey and egg. In a glass measuring cup, dissolve the baking soda in the ½ cup hot water. Gradually add one-half of the flour mixture to the syrup mix along with one-half of the hot water/soda and mix well. Stir in the remainder of the flour mixture and hot water/soda into the batter.

Pour into a greased round cake pan. Bake at 350 degrees for 30 minutes until cake springs when touched in the middle. The cake is good as a snacking cake; you may scatter remaining chocolate chips on top to melt, lightly dust with confectioner's sugar or add whipped topping.

Bibliography

Ancelet, Barry Jean, Jay Edwards and Glen Pitre. *Cajun Country*. Jackson: University Press of Mississippi, 1991.

Anderson, Brett. *Cornbread Nation 6: The Best of Southern Food Writing*. Athens: University of Georgia Press, 2012.

Anderson, Heather Arndt. *Breakfast: A History*. Lanham, MD: Altamira Press, 2013.

Angers, Trent. *The Truth about the Cajuns*. Lafayette, LA: Acadian House Publishing, 1989.

Ayto, John. *The Diner's Dictionary*. 2nd ed. Oxford, UK: Oxford University Press, 2012.

Bauer, Linda, and Steve Bauer. *Recipes from Historic Louisiana: Cooking with Louisiana's Finest Restaurants*. Albany, TX: Blue Sky Press, 2006.

Bienvenu, Marcelle, Carl A. Brasseaux and Ryan A. Brasseaux. *Stir the Pot: The History of Cajun Cuisine*. New York: Hippocrene Books, 2005.

Bowler, Gerry. *The World Encyclopedia of Christmas*. Toronto, ON: McClelland & Stewart Ltd., 2000.

Butler, W.E. *Down Among the Sugar Cane; The Story of Louisiana Sugar Plantations and Their Railroads*. Baton Rouge, LA: Moran Publishing Corporation, 1980.

Cajun Cuisine: Authentic Cajun Recipes from Louisiana's Bayou Country. Lafayette, LA: Beau Bayou Publishing Company, 1985.

D'Amico, Joan, and Karen Eich Drummond. *The U.S. History Cookbook*. Hoboken, NJ: John Wiley & Sons, 2003.

Dosier, Susan. *Civil War Cooking: The Confederacy*. Mankato, MN: Blue Earth Books, 2000.

Eagen, Rachel. *The Biography of Sugar*. New York: Crabtree Publishing, 2006.

Gioffre, Rosalba. *Fun with French Cooking*. New York: PowerKids Press, 2010.

Goldstein, Darra, ed. *The Oxford Companion to Sugar and Sweets*. Oxford, UK: Oxford University Press, 2015.

Guas, David, and Raquel Pelzel. *Dam Good Sweet*. Newton, CT: Taunton Press, 2009.

Gunderson, Mary. *Southern Plantation Cooking*. Mankato, MN: Blue Earth Books, 2000.

Gutierrez, C. Paige. *Cajun Foodways*. Jackson: University Press of Mississippi, 1992.

Herbst, Sharon Tyler. *The Deluxe Food Lover's Companion*. Hauppauge, NY: Barrons, 2009.

Humble, Nicola. *Cake: A Global History*. London: Reaktion Books, 2010.

Johnson, Pableaux. *Eating New Orleans: From French Quarter Creole Dining to the Perfect Poboy*. Woodstock, VT: Countryman Press, 2005.

Jones, Charlotte Foltz. *Eat Your Words*. New York: Delacorte Press, 1999.

Marks, Susan. *Finding Betty Crocker: The Secret Life of America's First Lady of Food*. New York: Simon & Schuster, 2005.

McCaffety, Kerri. *Etouffee, Mon Amour: The Great Restaurants of New Orleans*. Gretna, LA: Pelican Publishing Company, 2002.

Miller, Adrian. *Soul Food: The Surprising Story of an American Cuisine One Plate at a Time*. Chapel Hill: University of North Carolina Press, 2013.

Murphy, Michael. *Eat Dat New Orleans: A Guide to the Unique Food Culture of the Crescent City*. Woodstock, VT: Countryman Press, 2014.

O'Connell, Libby H. *The American Plate: A Culinary History*. Naperville, IL: Sourcebooks, 2014.

Robertson, Robin. *Rice & Spice*. Boston, MA: Harvard Common Press, 2000.

Sanson, Jerry Purvis. *Louisiana During World War II: Politics and Society, 1939–1945*. Baton Rouge: Louisiana State University Press, 1999.

Schenone, Laura. *A Thousand Years Over a Hot Stove*. New York: W.W. Norton & Company, 2003.

Shapiro, Laura. *Something from the Oven: Reinventing Dinner in 1950s America*. New York: Viking/The Penguin Group, 2004.

Staib, Walter. *A Sweet Taste of History*. Guilford, CT: Lyons Press, 2013.

Theophano, Janet. *Eat My Words: Reading Women's Lives Through the Cookbooks They Wrote*. New York: Palgrave, 2002.

Times-Picayune. *The Picayune's Creole Cookbook*. New York: Random House, 1987.

Tucker, Susan. *New Orleans Cuisine: Fourteen Signature Dishes and Their Histories*. Jackson: University Press of Mississippi, 2009.

Wohl, Kit. *New Orleans Classic Desserts*. Gretna, LA: Pelican Publishing Company, 2007.

Wuerthner, Terri Pischoff. *In a Cajun Kitchen; Authentic Cajun Recipes and Stories from a Family Farm on the Bayou*. New York: St. Martin's Press, 2006.

Index

About the Author

Dixie Poché is a graduate of the University of Louisiana–Lafayette in journalism. She is a travel and corporate writer in Lafayette and author of *Classic Eateries of Cajun Country*, published by American Palate, a division of The History Press. She enjoys doing research at the lunch counter and spends time with lots of Cajun cousins hanging out on the front porch.

Visit us at

www.historypress.net

CPSIA information can be obtained
at www.ICGtesting.com
Printed in the USA
LVHW080608220322
714062LV00004B/166